5-4-73

THIRD PRESS LIBRARY OF CRITICISM

General Editors: Joseph Okpaku and Luther Henkel

1
JAMES BALDWIN
A CRITICAL STUDY

JAMES BALDWIN

A CRITICAL STUDY

by Stanley Macebuh

THE THIRD PRESS
Joseph Okpaku Publishing Company, Inc.
444 Central Park West, New York, N.Y. 10025

Library of Congress Catalogue Card Number: LC 72–93679
SBN 89388–064–7

First printing

Designed by Bennie Arrington

1744888

For M.M.
With Love

ACKNOWLEDGMENTS

For the use of copyright material in this book the publishers are grateful to the following:

Twayne Publishers, Inc., for permission to quote from the poem: 'Dark Symphony', 1953, by Melvin Tolson;

Beacon Press, for permission to quote from *Notes of a Native Son,* 1964, by James Baldwin;

M. Evans & Co., Inc., for permission to quote from *The Furious Passage of James Baldwin,* © 1966, by Fern Marja Eckman;

Doubleday & Co., Inc., for permission to quote from *The Black Aesthetic,* 1971, by Addison Gayle;

Signet Books, for permission to quote from *Invisible Man,* 1952, and *Shadow and Act,* 1966, both by Ralph Ellison;

Harper and Row, for permission to quote from *Perspectives in Contemporary Criticism,* 1968, by S. N. Grebstein, and *Native Son,* 1966, by Richard Wright;

Dell Publishing Co., Inc., for permission to quote from the following titles, all by James Baldwin: *Go Tell It on the Mountain,* 1953, *Giovanni's Room,* 1956, *The Fire Next Time,* 1962, *Tell Me How Long the Train's Been Gone,* 1967, and *Going to Meet the Man,* 1965;

Dial Press, for permission to quote from the following, all by James Baldwin: *Nobody Knows My Name,* 1961, *Another Country,* 1963, and *No Name in the Street,* 1972;

Astor-Honor, Inc., for permission to quote from *Things Fall Apart,* 1959, by Chinua Achebe;

Everett Edwards, for permission to quote from *The Black American Writer: Vol. 1, Fiction,* 1969;

Christianity and Crisis, for permission to quote from an article entitled "Beyond White Theology" by Reuben Sheares. Reprinted from the Nov. 2 and 16, 1970 issues of *Christianity and Crisis,* copyright © 1970 by Christianity and Crisis, Inc.

Preface

The following study was undertaken both as a labour of love and as part of an act of expiation. We who were born in Africa had been, until recently, a little too complacent, a little too willing to accept our predicament in a world torn by racial lines merely as existential fact. We had been too ready to suppose that there was too much of hysterical posturing to the struggle of our cousins here, a posturing that we thought, alas, led to the loss of that intrinsic dignity of which we believed we were the last custodians in a world gone mad with moral vulgarity. We had, of course, the comforting advantage of distance, far removed as we were, we thought, from the hate that threatened to plunge the world into oblivion. Events of the last decade proved our elegant self-congratulation to have been fanciful, and we were therefore forced into a process of introspection to which we were hardly accustomed.

James Baldwin was one of those who guided me through the peculiar traumas of blackness. He was, for me, the most difficult black writer in all the world, and to attempt to understand him was to attempt to comprehend my own delusions. The study that follows is therefore as much a personal testament as it is an analysis of the writings of this most annoying of writers. Hesitancies probably abound here, but those I recognised I have chosen to leave in, since I believe that the critical task is ultimately impossible of divorcement from the emotions, prejudices, and also, illusions of those who engage in it.

My task has been to examine the record of Baldwin's development both as writer and thinker. I suggest that he is at his technical best when he is dealing with personal, more or less autobiographical realities; that the significant dynamic of this reality is his haunting sense of theological danger; that before he could discover an authentic public voice, which he appeared to have been aiming for, he had first to come to terms with his dread of Hell, but that having finally found this voice, his ability to accommodate it within a plausible and effective fictional framework appears to have been compromised. I then go on to suggest that he will be remembered not so much for the structural and 'aesthetic' competence of his earlier novels, but for the moral authority and intense passion of his more recent writings. It is well to add here, however, that this is by no means a reliable biography of James Baldwin, since I have generally made use of biographical information only to clarify certain issues and problems in his works.

To those who contributed to this study, my gratitude; but since they will probably recognise themselves in it, I need not mention their names here. To my students, both at the University of California in Berkeley, and at the City College in New York, who are probably too humble to recognise an idea taken here and there, from their term papers, I shall forever be indebted, not only for their vigorous and healthy scepticisms, in the particular case of Baldwin, but for their readiness also to tolerate my by no means comprehensive knowledge of actual, as distinct from imaginary creative situations. One hopes they will see here an honest search for meaning, but if they are disappointed by the mood of this book, it will be but part of the price that we, the accidental Africans of this century, will continue to pay for the crime of our fathers. . . . *Delicta maiorum lues. . . .*

S. M.
New York, 1973

Contents

One

Introduction

A basic assumption in this study is that the criticism of Black Literature in America sorely needs at this time an approach that is at once serious, useful, and sustained. There is no lack of commentary on the subject, but quite often it is not at all clear from the views expressed what the critical presuppositions are that have led to the conclusions presented. The evolution of the concept of the Black Aesthetic has in recent years made it possible for black writers and critics to base their views on a reasonably cogent critical standard, but many of the establishment critics still appear, in the main, to be groping for a set of critical propositions that could be applied to what some of them claim is unfamiliar literature. Such, at any rate, is the general situation at the moment, that observations made on the subject appear often to be more significant as vague sentiment than as excursions into meaningful criticism of individual writers and their works. It is part of the intention of this book, therefore, to suggest, with Baldwin as example, one way in which the situation may be corrected. The primary emphasis here is on detailed analysis of his works, and in particular his novels, though in Chapter Six we have thought it necessary to attempt to place him firmly within a tradition in Black Literature to which he so eminently belongs. But in order to provide a useful perspective for the particular conclusions reached here, it is well to begin with a brief examination of the critical situation as it exists at the present time.

Total acceptance by white Americans of the black experience in the United States may or may not be, as Baldwin and others have argued, the one condition upon which rests the survival of American culture, but it does seem clear now that Black Literature fully promises to be one body of writings that has the potential of determining the future probity of American criticism. If one may go by Theodore Gross' observations on the matter[1], there is hardly an American critic or teacher of literature who has not had to contend with the web of issues posed for criticism by Black Literature in this country; the days are presumably gone when interest in it was something of an after-dinner entertainment whose primary value lay in its supposed exoticism. Few Americans can any longer pretend not to be aware of the significance of racism in their culture, and consequently the shock of recognition has led to a spate of critical outpourings that have ranged from the occasionally impressive to the preponderantly trivial. Since widespread critical concern with this literature is a phenomenon only of recent years, one may consider the volume of the interest in it a welcome development in American critical history; but it must also be observed that there has been, so far, a disturbing gap between an apparently mandatory interest in the subject and a less than distinguished critical response to it.

There appears to be a vague uneasiness, in much of the discussion on the subject, that it exists somewhere in limbo, hovering between the grandiosely insignificant and the implausibly eschatological. Apart from those, like David Littlejohn, who coyly believe that there is an inartistic and monotonous persistence of the theme of racial injustice in this literature, a typical excuse for this attitude appears often to be that, in dealing with a literature as contemporary and topical as Black Literature, the critic is obliged to exercise a good deal of caution. Criticism, Bacon once said, is the application of reason to the imagination, but in the current critical parlance, reason has become quite indistinguishable from caution, a caution, too, that is dictated not by humility, but by the calculated desire to avoid controversy. Such in any case is the attendant corruption of the Baconian counsel that the critic who would normally pride himself on the possession of a 'liberal imagination' ends up often, in his response to Black Literature, a helpless victim of the irrational influence of racism in American culture[2].

In more specific terms, the caution we here refer to is sometimes indicated in the preoccupation of many critics with issues of critical procedure, as an end in itself—who should be given the privilege of commenting on Black Literature, whether or not the term is itself a specious one, whether the theme of racial injustice is a fit subject for serious art. It can hardly be doubted that certain ground rules need to be established for critical concern with this literature, but preoccupation with rules is in itself of negligible significance if it is not frankly regarded as a tool, a means of rational and meaningful elucidation of actual content. There are those who have questioned the legitimacy of this literature as anything more than 'writing by Negroes', and doubting its validity as a category recognisably separate from the mainstream of American letters, have found in this demurral a fit justification for avoiding so vibrant a body of writing. A few others have been willing to admit its legitimacy, but have been unduly parsimonious in recognising its achievements. We do not intend to take issue here with the literary integrationists; they would presumably be ready to do battle, also, with D. H. Lawrence, who probably began the process by which American letters acquired the respectability of a national literature separate from its European prototype. Our major concern is with the patronising obfuscations implicit in the attitude of those who, while accepting the legitimacy of Black Literature, have yet been either unwilling to, or incapable of offering any consistent or plausible justification for their faith.

Such critics rightly argue that in certain fundamental respects the criteria that govern criticism of Black Literature need to be different, for instance, from those that apply to the criticism of a Jamesian novel, but it often appears that the reasons they adduce for this position, the development of their major conclusion, hardly ever touch the crux of the matter. The point is that black writing in America has never really been, to borrow a well-worn phrase, the indulgent diversion of a bored leisure class. It has not been distinguished, until quite recently, for its preoccupation with questions of 'aesthetics', nor, in the matter of content, has a compulsive concern with 'universal' themes been one of its significant characteristics. If Harry Levin is right in suggesting that Western art has characteristically oscillated between the 'Byzantine' impulse toward symbol-

3

ism and the more 'western' concern with 'the development of human individuality'[3], it seems clear that Black Literature in America has hardly ever followed this pattern. Jean Toomer and Ralph Ellison may have attempted in their writings to discover an appropriate balance between the symbolic and the realistic, and William Melvin Kelley may have given indication in *A Different Drummer*, of a certain theoretical concern with the problem of allegory in art, but their particular definition of the problem that required solution in actual practice is by no means representative of the typical concern of the black writer in America. With the necessary exception of folklore, of course, the Thomist concept of 'figuration' in art, that process, deriving from Saint Paul and Saint Augustine, whereby the literal meaning of a work of art may be extended into various levels of increasing significance (and which is not to be confused with the code-like notion of 'signifying' in black culture) has hardly ever been considered a meaningful artistic technique in Black Literature. But from this medieval concept of figuration arose one of the central issues in Western art of the modern period, namely, the supposed conflict between symbolism and realism; and it is an indication of the oddity of Black Literature in America that it cannot usefully be cited in illustration of this conflict. It is not that the black writer has been oblivious of the power of symbols, and the meticulous researcher will no doubt be quite successful in discovering isolated cases in which the black writer has relied heavily on 'emblems' and 'signs' in his art. But it does seem reasonable to suggest that in general, the very nature of his experience has tended to preclude the sort of preoccupation with symbols, with that extreme conceptualisation of image that led the Symbolist School to suppose that the world we live in is but an imperfect representation of a superior world of which the artist is the legitimate interpreter. Rinehart's tinted glasses in Ellison's *Invisible Man* might conceivably be understood both as sign and emblem, but it is equally clear that whatever meaning they may have is firmly rooted in the actual experience of man in society, and not in some version of an other-worldly reality. Even in the case of Baldwin, where we are clearly presented with a far more theological, even medieval vision of corruption and salvation, the experience

4

presented is most often more significant as phenomenal reality than as the allegorical prefiguration of a world beyond ours. In effect, then, one of the dominant moods in Black Literature in America appears to be a preoccupation not with heaven but with the visible world, with the traumas of reality.

Harry Levin argues in the essay mentioned above that

> . . . in times which seem to be out of joint, when man is alienated from his environment, the heroic seems less attainable and love itself may dim to a Platonic vision. A failure of nerve is accompanied by a retreat from reality[4].

Now, the concept of the 'heroic' in significant Black Literature in this country is neither 'classical' nor Shakespearean. Our hero is seldom a Ulysses or an Aeneas, nor, when his end is tragic, is he often granted the privilege of elegant selfknowledge. He usually dies violently and prematurely, without even the promise of transcendence and growth in wisdom. His heroism stems, typically, from the strife and turbulence of his experience. His conception of love is decidedly un-Platonic, indeed visceral; he cannot afford to suffer from a 'failure of nerve' because the most likely consequence of this is not merely a 'retreat from reality', but, quite simply, death. If our reading of the situation is at all plausible, it seems clear, then, that one way of identifying the difference between Black Literature and 'Western' Literature in general is by considering the varying strategies of accommodation that the black and Western writer have typically employed against their sense of 'alienation'. Where the black writer is *born* alienated, the Western writer is likely to discover his alienation in his maturity, by a deliberate act, as it were, of meditation. Richard Wright's Outsider notwithstanding, the typical black hero is more likely to go along, a little dazed, with Ellison's Invisible Man and insist that

> . . . live you must, and you can either make passive love to your sickness or burn it out and go on to the next conflicting phase.

5

On the other hand, our contemporary view of the typical figure in Western Literature is of the man who either pointlessly awaits the return of Godot, or with the battle cry of that pitiable fellow in James Purdy's *Malcolm* cries out, 'Keep your hands off my soul' and then retreats into the cult of individualism. Where questions of personal identity have tended for most other writers to be of more or less philosophical or aesthetic significance, the issue has for the black writer tended to assume an all-important immediacy, since it has had everything to do with his very survival as a social being. Once the stark immediacy of this actual situation is assumed, it becomes clear that excellence òf literary form is not going to be construed as an end in itself—the black writer faced with the problem of how to accommodate his experience is not likely to construe the aesthetic process as the principal object of his creative endeavour, nor is he likely to be obsessed with writing the Great American Novel. Rather, the creative imagination will become for him no more than a vehicle of self-assertion in a world that has conspired to deny meaning to his life, and the principles of criticism will in turn have less to do with discovering the mimetic approximations of nature's beauty than with the applicability of the vision of life presented in art. In other words, even for the most alienated Western writer, whether he retreats behind an undecipherable wall of symbolism or of Kafkaesque absurdity, or even into the cult of individualism, there is nearly always an at least theoretical presumption of an earlier time (Hellenic, Renaissance, Elizabethan, or, in America, even pre-Civil War Southern), an Arcadian age when God was in his Heaven and all was well on earth; for if God is indeed dead, he must be presumed to have been at some point manifestly alive. And the state of mind that is induced by an albeit traumatic sense of loss is not nearly to be compared with that anger that stems from the conviction of the primordial conspiracy of the cosmos. For, as Leslie Fiedler points out in a different context, one source of the black man's radical and angry sense of alienation derived historically from the impossibility of translating his experience in Africa either into the language or mores of his slave-masters in America. For him, modern history begins with slavery, and he was compelled to travel backward beyond time, as it were, if he

6

was to recall an even mythically ideal Golden Age. His white counterpart could express his sense of loss in the same language (if not with the same emphasis) which his forefathers used, but the black American could not, until quite recently, even begin to talk reasonably about a 'sense of loss', since that which was American about his history was but an unmitigated record of misery and absurdity.

It may reasonably be surmised that the attitude to life of such a man as we have tried here to characterize is going to be quite different, in intention at any rate, from that of the man who has a body of unbroken and usable historical legend to fall back on. Sartre's Antoine Roquentin in *La Nausée* can afford to retreat into the imaginary world of art because his historical intelligence suggests to him that this is a plausible alternative; but Ralph Ellison's Invisible Man can only 'hibernate' for a while, soon to re-emerge into the world of active engagement, for he knows that the only meaningful alternative to this is, not philosophical dalliance, nor the elegant but nonetheless meretricious declaration of a separate peace, but the inevitable suicide of Baldwin's Rufus in *Another Country*. Neither the 'Byzantine' retreat into symbolism, then, nor the consolations of philosophy and aesthetics will be particularly meaningful as alternatives for the black confronted by so peculiar an experience, and it is in this context worth remembering, for instance, that the response of most black Americans to the philosophical expression of existentialism has always been one of slightly patronizing tolerance; and this not because it was thought to be an implausible outlook on life (indeed the record suggests that it has had some attraction for such differing sensibilities as Wright's and Ellison's) but because, when advocated by the professional thinkers, it invariably took on the contours of just another intellectual fad, only remotely linked to the realities of their advocates' lives[5].

Fantasy and escapism are by no means unknown elements in the actual lives of black people in America, but the significant literature that presents and interprets this life is, surprisingly, firmly rooted in realism. And it is in the context of the general failure to recognise this perspective of realism that we may most usefully consider the issue of 'protest' in black American Literature. To the extent that any creative writer seeks not merely to present an encapsulated 'picture' of experience but attempts also to re-order the chaos of reality, he is, of course, engaged in protest against that which exists. Indeed, there is a sense in which all art may be seen as protest by virtue of its most characteristic intent not merely to offer a duplication, but quite often a radical revision of the world we know through our senses. And in this sense *Madame Bovary*, *A Portrait of the Artist*, and *A Farewell to Arms* may all be seen as belonging in the same family as *Native Son*. But when David Littlejohn stigmatizes what he sees as the unfortunate persistence of the theme of protest in black American Literature[6], it is clearly not this sense that he has in mind. What he has in mind is much more tangible, having to do with that vision of life which Richard Gilman was later to characterize as 'absolute theme and necessity' for the black writer; his objection is not against 'protest', but against the black writer's 'preoccupation' with racism in American life. But the triviality of his position becomes quite staggering when it is considered that the only meaningful alternative open to the black writer is the retreat into 'symbolism' and eery fantasy, a process that Harry Levin assures us is an unmistakable symptom of cultural decadence. If Bellow, Salinger and Mailer demonstrate a radical discomfiture over the nature and quality of modern life, we can hardly expect the black writer who wishes to remain honest to his experience to become the laureate of the age of affluence, for as Chester Himes aptly suggests in his autobiography, the most authentic quality of the black writer's life is not 'alienation', certainly not the complacency of affluence, but a seemingly inescapable hurt. In terms of his aesthetic responsibility, therefore, to record this hurt is, as it were, to retain a certain minimum of sanity, to keep his feet firmly upon the ground of his unique experience.

With due regard to those who would immediately retort that pain and suffering are universal themes in literature, it is worth observing that if art is a criticism of life, Black Literature in America has been the most dramatic justification of this in recent times. And it is not necessary to draw attention to writers like Baldwin or LeRoi Jones to illustrate this assertion: the very existence of the American black has always been a moral and social criticism—in the most specific meaning of the term—of life in America. And if, then, Black Literature is the mirror of American life, it may be expected that the critical response to it will often reflect the uneasiness, the fears and the feelings of guilt that such exposures normally engender; and this, it would appear, is what has happened. Mike Thelwell, in a not so recent review of Baldwin's *Another Country*, argues that

> . . . sometimes it chances that the critical response to a work of fiction will reveal as much about the society that produced that work, as the work of fiction itself. *Another Country* has proved to be such a work: too important to ignore and too cruelly honest and threatening to deal with objectively. At least this seems to have been the experience of some of our most prestigious critics[7].

Objectivity in critical approaches to Black Literature has tended to be only an occassional, if not downright impossible virtue, but in general Mr. Thelwell's observations are even more pertinent today than when they were written. Contemporary Black Literature is a literature of intense engagement, of energetic involvement both for the writer and the reader, and despite the varying subterfuges which such writers as Ellison and Baldwin have had to adopt, the former with his syncretism of form, the latter with his attempts to expand the limits of protest in art, its major theme has always been one of outrage, an attempt to accommodate the anger and the despair of which the black writer, especially, has had to be the recorder. If, therefore, this literature embodies in a more concentrated form that element of criticism that is thought to be the realm of art, it seems reasonable to expect that useful responses to it will have to go beyond the feverish search for not so obvious analogies and models. Where a literature as dynamic and topical as this is concerned, in a literature to which the Wordsworthian precept of emotion recollected in tranquility hardly ever seems to apply, in which there is but a thin line separating art from historical reality, 'formal' criticism, by which we mean the criticism of genres and techniques simply will not do. Serious interest in it will have to admit frankly that its responsibility goes beyond even intelligent analysis of form, beyond sophisticated definitions, and embraces

9

moral, political and philosophical evaluation of the writer's imagination at work.

It would perhaps be useful here to illustrate the confusion that appears to be so inseparable a part of the critical response to Black Literature by referring briefly to Richard Gilman's 1968 essay, 'White Standards and Negro Writers' [8]. His major claim to our attention appears to rest upon a public confession of inadequacy of experience in dealing with 'black literature', on account of which we are expected, presumably, to congratulate him for avoiding that superciliousness which so many of his profession have shown in regard to this subject. Because it takes a certain kind of courage to make this confession in a field in which such admissions are rare, his humility has the initial advantage of disarming his readers, since, if they are black, they would be less likely to be critical of anyone who makes such modest claims for himself. But for those interested as much in the details of his argument as in his final proposal, it would appear that his initial advantage is lost in the maze of confusion and double-talk that characterize his essay. It is true that he shows a certainly unusual enthusiasm for what he calls 'black writing', describing it with consummate eloquence; but concealed beneath this enthusiasm are two major assumptions, so insidious in their implications that they ultimately expose his prescription for white critics as being in fact no more adequate than the attitudes he himself dismisses as hypocritical.

Consider, first of all, his inexplicably ambiguous attitude to Black Literature. He assures us that he will go on "elucidating novels and plays and poetry by Negroes", but that any writing that does not fall within any of these categories, any writing that demonstrates "the act of creation of the self in the face of that self's historic denial by our society", is beyond the limits of his competence[9]. He considers himself eminently qualified to deal with black novels, plays and poems, apparently because they belong to neatly compartmentalised, familiar categories, whereas the 'new' type of writing, say, by Cleaver, is almost entirely unrecognisable to him. The fundamental issue involved in this claim is an obvious one. What Gilman seeks to establish is a clear dichotomy between the sensibility that informs the work of writers like Baldwin or Ellison and that of others like Cleaver or Malcolm X. The qualitative difference for him, between Ellison and Baldwin on the one hand, and Cleaver on the other, appears to be the supposition that the former are "imaginative writers who produce fictions, however autobiographical these may appear, works of literary art. . . .", whereas Cleaver has never written a novel, play or poem. According to him, then, neither *Native Son* nor *Invisible Man* demonstrates the 'act of creation of the self', nor do these novels seek to reassert the humanity of the black man in a world that has striven to deny meaning to his life. But what precisely, it may be asked, makes Gilman so certain he is in a position to elucidate *Native Son* in any way that can be considered adequate? If he is reluctant to pass judgment on *Soul on Ice*, is *Another Country* so bland and objectified a work of 'literary art' that he can feel comfortable with it? Or is it because in his complacent preoccupation with genres and forms he has failed to pay sufficient attention to the devastating content of these novels? Once these questions are asked, it becomes clear that what Gilman would have us believe is an honest reluctance to pontificate over unfamiliar material does in fact carry with it the much more serious charge of a level of confusion that goes far beyond the limits of his own genteel confessions. To seek to draw a distinction between Cleaver's *Soul on Ice* and black 'novels, plays and poems' merely on the basis of what appears to be a difference in *form* is to be guilty of the same perverseness of which he accuses the white literary establishment. For if blackness is, with Cleaver, 'absolute theme and necessity', so also is it for Baldwin, and even, also, for Ellison, and this in spite of the different forms in which they choose to express themselves. Despite the mediations of 'art' (and we are not at all persuaded that Cleaver's book is as artless as Gilman seems to think it is) there is an integrity of vision, a unity of general perspective evident in all these works, whether literary or autobiographical, that involves them ultimately in an identical tradition. In other words, though this has given rise to some academic inquiry, the essay form, in the hands of a Cleaver, a Baldwin, or a Malcolm X, is just as much an art form as the novel or poem or play, precisely because, in black American literature, the mood and its expression are more important than the medium of expression.

One general issue raised here is whether in fact it is at all useful to speak of black art in the same manner that one speaks of Western or European art, but ultimately the matter resolves itself into the questions as to whether Cleaver's book, which Gilman uses as his example, may be regarded as 'literature' or not; yet even from the perspective of 'art', it should not have been so difficult for him to discover that *Soul on Ice*, if considered as an integral whole rather than as a collection of essays, depends for its effectiveness only partially upon statistically provable evidence, or on the kind of systematic exposition that we usually associate with non-artistic works, and that both in its attempt to provide a viable myth for the black American and in the power of Cleaver's imagination, it belongs as much to the 'literature' of black America as Baldwin's *The Fire Next Time*.

There is, however, a second presumption in Gilman's essay that we would like to touch upon here. It is now often thought that the 'philosophy' of America's young men and women, the world of the 'under-thirties', is one that is largely unintelligible to the older citizens of this country. The young tend to be less 'rational', more emotional in their behaviour; their social and political attitudes, where these are given verbal form, tend to be syncretic, deriving from no exclusive tradition, but appropriating the whole of the known history of mankind as their source of inspiration. Both in their mythology and their pantheon of heroes, one does not notice any unambiguous influences from a Newman or a Henry Adams, but we are not aware that anyone has seriously accused them of being anything but 'Western' in their fundamental assumptions about life. Given the sense of outrage which their detractors feel, it seems clear that one basic cause of the rift is the younger generation's use, or abuse, of language. Language, or the absence of it, thus becomes, for those who would protect America from internal corrosion, the symbol of everything they object to. It is not that the young are incapable of intelligent expression (they are certainly better educated than their fathers) nor that the language they speak is different, in its basic form, from that of their critics; where their language is considered objectionable therefore, it is not usually because those who consider it so cannot *understand*, but because they understand it only too well. And so the level of contention revolves not so much around the use of language, as around the implications of the right which the young appear to arrogate to themselves to return to more 'fundamental' usages; for those, for instance, who prefer a less pretentious word for 'sexual intercourse', are the same who would return to the pristine virtues that America is thought once to have possessed in almost exclusive abundance. Ultimately, then, it is plausible to argue that one basic factor in the response of the 'silent majority' is, not a failure of comprehension, but fear, fear that those who revel in verbal innocence are a threat to the foundations of Western culture (in its present American version). And once the issue is seen in this light, it becomes clear that the battle is being fought, not between two totally different cultures, but between interpretations of the same culture—a crisis that is nothing if not symptomatic of the historic tensions in Western civilization.

And if this is true of the confrontation between the young and the not-young in America, it is also true of the confrontation between black and white. The black man's mythology is different, and necessarily so, because the details of his social experience are different; his pantheon of heroes is intensely functional, his language equally symbolic of his rebellion against the mainstream. Yet just as the silent majority cannot pretend not to understand their children, it seems equally irrational to ask for a suspension of judgment by white critics merely on the grounds that the black man's historic predicament in America is totally unintelligible to white America. What is at stake is not really whether Gilman understands Eldridge Cleaver, but whether the white critic is prepared to make the effort to overcome what appears to be a psychological reluctance to examine himself and his countrymen on the basis of the evidence which he confronts in reading Cleaver. *If* you do not need to be a homosexual in order to understand Genet's world (and Gilman claims you do not) you equally do not need to be black to read Cleaver profitably. While, therefore, it is true that in certain fundamental respects the black experience in America has been utterly different from the white, it would be a fallacy to conclude from this that it in some way grants the white critic absolution from responsible, honest and intelligent self-confrontation.

It need hardly be said that our observations here are not by any means limited exclusively to the issues raised by black literature in America, but it must also be remarked that the white critic can hardly congratulate himself in the discharge of his responsibilities were he to adopt Gilman's counsels of strategic reticence. But if it is true that the white critic has, in general, evinced a not-too-useful preoccupation with procedures (when, that is, he is not engaged in decrying the obsessive persistence of racial themes in black literature) his black counterpart has sometimes, also, approached his responsibilities with a degree of defensiveness that is, in our opinion, symptomatic of the same uneasiness. The black critical response to William Styron's *The Confessions of Nat Turner* is a case in point[10]. It would be a fair summary of the critics' response to this novel to say that, in general, their outrage is motivated by what they consider the historical distortions of Styron's novel, the fact that he insinuates that Nat Turner was a homosexual, that his revolutionary fervour was vitiated by a somewhat morbid infatuation with an ethereal, rather over-poeticized white female character, that in the end he showed a rather unrevolutionary abhorrence of violence. And in identifying the numerous falsifications and suggestive silences, they tend to argue that it was part of Styron's mythopoeic exercise to suggest that a black revolution in America was bound to fail, whether then or now, precisely because the black revolutionary's inevitable fascination with the white female would always prove his ultimate nemesis. We do not mean to suggest that this is the only opinion held by black writers and thinkers (Baldwin's own response was certainly much more complimentary to Styron) nor do we contend that the critics' identification of Styron's distortions is out of place. For obviously *The Confessions* does raise certain fundamental questions regarding the uses and limitations of the historical novel that we need not go into here. But it does seem that in thus confining themselves to questioning the credibility of Styron's flirtations with history, they overlooked a much more important responsibility that has to do with examining the very validity of Styron's own conclusions. Since, by his own admission, the novel was something of an exercise in applied history, an attempt, often more implied than stated, to find some explanation for the

14

contemporary black revolutionary consciousness, its chances of success, a more pertinent question would be, to what extent can it be considered true that the revolutionary hero has the obligation at once to provide public, inspirational leadership and a private moral example for his followers? Even granting that the black man has always to come to terms with the private demon of his alleged sexual infatuation with the white female (and this is a conclusion that is implicit in Styron's novel) by what process of reasoning can the abjuration of this fantasy be seen as a necessary and sufficient condition for the success of his struggle? Since when did homosexuality, or even heterosexual infatuations become, not just a matter of putative abnormality, but a tragic, ethical flaw that necessarily foredooms the efforts of the revolutionary hero?

Such questions as we have here asked are in some sense obviously extra-literary, but since it is part of our argument that the critical response to blackness has to deal with much more than its formal, literary characteristics, they are quite pertinent here. Rather than limit themselves to the question of the reliability of Styron's uses of history, the contributors to this collection of essays would have done much better to take up Styron on his own terms, and to question the very plausibility, even granting the truth of his evidence, of his conclusions. In the end what they seem to have achieved is the clearly unintended implication that had Styron's historical data been correct, his conclusions would necessarily have been valid. Nor, again, is this defensiveness confined to the black response to Styron's novel. It is, for instance, suggestive that discussions on the achievement of black leaders in this country, whether by whites or blacks (and this is of particular importance with regard to responses to Baldwin) often tend to end up in evaluations, both implicit and explicit, of the moral probity of their private lives. Obviously, there is a case for arguing that leadership implies an invitation to the invasion of one's privacy, and it is presumably reasonable to expect that he who would lead his fellow men assumes the obligation of a degree of rectitude in his private life that would perhaps not be expected of his followers. But it would be misleading to assume from this that there is a necessary and inevitable connection between the probity of a leader's private morals and the effectiveness of his public leadership. It is therefore one of the basic flaws of Styron's novel that he appears to insist on this connection to the extent that he seems to attribute the failure of Nat Turner's rebellion, not to the overwhelming social odds against him, but to Turner's sexual fantasies. That this temptation to predicate the quality of public leadership upon some notion of private moral rectitude is a widespread one is perhaps exemplified by John Williams' recent book on Martin Luther King. Williams' major thesis seems to be that King's significance as a leader lay more in his promise than in his actual achievement; but it is also part of his argument that the gap between the moral fervour of King's public role and the rumoured improprieties of his private life was a trap that exposed him to potential exploitation by the white establishment. In fairness to Williams it must be said that he does not appear entirely to believe these rumours (though he attaches appreciably more significance to them than does one of King's more reliable biographers)[11]; but he also seems to wish they had not existed, or at any rate that they had not been known to the powers in Washington, and the implication here is that these rumours had something to do with what he sees as the tragic ambiguity of King's actual achievement.

The King God Didn't Save[12] may not be imaginative literature, though there are elements in it that suggest the approach to history of a creative writer—notice, for instance, the very format of the last chapters of the book, in which commentary on factual information is interspersed with what can only be termed unverifiable gossip, both nonetheless coalescing to provide a much more complex portrait of King's character. But Williams' *The Man Who Cried I Am* is literature, even by Gilman's exclusive standards, and if there is a single black novel that illustrates the plausibility of our argument that the criticism of 'forms' is inadequate as an approach to black literature, it would have to be this novel. *The Man Who Cried I Am* is the perfect example of a novel whose ultimate significance goes quite beyond the issue of the author's formal, 'aesthetic' achievement. From the perspective of plot, the rectal disease that foredooms Max Reddick's life represents a flaw in conception that diminishes the sacrificial significance of his death; and, again,

Williams' narrative method in this novel, functionally appropriate though it may be in suggesting the basic rootlessness of the American black, his endless wanderings in search of a locale to which he could feel spiritually attached, yet carries with it the insinuation of a hastily assembled travelogue, in which geographical details of, at best, trivial importance are at times made to serve as rather poor substitutes for serious delineation of character. In reading this novel, one sometimes gets the feeling that Williams is interested as much in demonstrating his seasoned traveller's knowledge of strange places as in telling a meaningful story, and we suspect that some readers will find the very bulk of this novel somewhat intimidating. From the perspective of plot and narrative method, then, it may well be that this is not Williams' best effort so far, but whatever its technical faults, these are more than compensated for by the vision that informs this novel. In many ways the creative response to Harold Cruse's devastating tirade against the black 'intellectual', *The Man Who Cried* seeks, it would appear, to evaluate the role of the black intellectual in the continuing struggle and to suggest a strategy of involvement that could bridge the perennial gap that separates him from mass man (black).

Max Reddick and Harry Ames are representatives of the black American intellectual whose desire to liberate their fellow blacks is often predicated upon their tragic awareness of almost predetermined failure. Minister Q is the proletarian spokesman who, without the accoutrements of intellectual subtlety, yet is more successful in articulating the aspirations of the common man. In practical terms, the possibility of cooperation between them is extremely remote, partly because, in 'class' terms, Max and Harry belong to a different group from that which Minister Q represents, but also because it is part of the intellectual habit to be conscious of those complexities in life which, whatever their objective validity, do tend to diminish the chances of positive commitment. Where, for instance, Minister Q recognises the certainty of impending assassination as a fact to be accepted with a certain wry sense of humour[13], for Max the possibility that he could lay down his life for the cause is something of a revelation, the end result, as it were, of a long period of meditation. Ultimately, of course, both Max and Harry and

Minister Q do die at the hands of the agents of the white establishment, because the secret information they possess is too explosive to be left with them. But the significance of Williams' creative achievement in this novel lies not so much in the fact that these men have to die fighting for the same cause as in Max's final vision of the possibility of providing the missing link, the chain that would bind him, as a representative of the intellectual community, to the masses. And it is precisely this vision, this dream of an indestructible 'chain', that alters what would merely have been just another inconclusive essay in the ramifications of political strategy into a serious creative statement of possibilities. For the true meaning of Max's final gesture lies more in the realm of possibilities than of actual fact; Minister Q dies, and in practical terms the details of the King Alfred Plan die with him. But we are persuaded that there are those to whom he has passed on this information who would escape the most untiring attentions of the Intelligence agencies precisely because they are anonymous, and who would continue the struggle. Max and Minister Q may die, the novelist appears to be saying, but the fight goes on. Revolutions need leaders, but they also need and are initiated on behalf of ordinary men, the men of the twilight cafes and dim-lighted streets. And Max actually begins *to be* only after he recognises that his intellectualisations need be, not a source of alienation from the people, but the very agent of his reunification with them. That the idea of the chain of complementary responsibilities that binds all black people together is an important one for Mr. Williams is further demonstrated by his recent assessment of Dr. King. For him, King was historically simply another point in the chain of leaders that must go on until the end of the struggle, but where, in his biography, he presents this idea in explicit terms[14], the idea of the 'chain' is, appropriately enough, more implied than stated in *The Man Who Cried*.

Our comments on this novel have obviously not been exhaustive, but they are sufficient to suggest that it would be futile merely to confine oneself to an assessment of Williams' achievement as a producer of 'literary art'. From a strictly artistic point of view, the novel does suffer from certain technical flaws, deriving both from the questionable aproppriateness of Max's anal disease and from the constant and apparently aimless juggling with geographical focus, but, as with many other contemporary black novels, the technical framework is only a functional medium, and certainly has no more important a place in the overall achievement than the subject dealt with. In this case it is possible to argue that the very immediacy and gravity of the problem which Williams deals with here, his attempt to provide a creative solution to the 'crisis' of the black intellectual, tends to render any preoccupation with technical criticism somewhat frivolous. In the end, of course, one would have to come to some judgment as to the plausibility of the particular vision of unity presented in this novel, but that would be beyond the scope of this chapter.

Black American literature, particularly in its contemporary versions, provides for the responsible critic both a challenge and a temptation. To deal with it adequately, he needs to recognise both that his subject encompasses a world that is often more real than the world of his normal endeavours, and that in a profession in which the search for objectivity is often an excuse for moral lethargy, integrity of approach is a much more attainable objective. It would, we dare say, be flattering to many blacks that a critic of Gilman's stature should recommend that his fellow white critics exercise considerable caution in dealing with black literature, but one must warn against the danger that this may turn out to be just another fashionable excuse for the suspension, not only of public judgment, but also of honest, private reflection. The tensions in American society are today too strident for anyone to claim not to be aware of what is going on, and criticism does offer one of the less painful opportunities for self-examination. Judicious silence may, on occasion, be a rare virtue, but critical silence that is based on the questionable claim of incomprehension is obviously undesirable at this point in time.

But if critical silence is undesirable, there is little reason to believe that undeliberated critical assertions are any more useful. We may suppose, with Edward Spriggs, that the black creative writer possesses something of an a priori, unassailable prophetic autonomy—

19

Pray not for-the Poet
Saints,
Pray instead,
Saints, for his critics[15]

—but it would hardly be an intelligent exercise of judgment to presume that the black critic can lay an equally meaningful claim to
the poet's privilege of 'divine arrogance'. It is, sometimes, of the essence of the writer's role that he may simply assert without any attempt either to clarify or to justify his assertions, and it is certainly
plausible to argue, as Carolyn Gerald has, that the artist often operates on a level that is 'intuitive, deep beyond the threshold of reason and common sense'. But one can hardly conceive of a state of
affairs in which the responsible critic arrogates to himself a role
thus analogous to the writer's. We may have reached, it is true, a
point in contemporary literature where the role of the artist is, almost by definition, quite beyond criticism, a point where the critic
has long been superannuated without knowing it[16]; but assuming
that the critic still has a valid function to discharge, one can hardly
suppose that his role is anything as elevated or glamorous as the
artist's. Where the artist can, and does often achieve his purpose
precisely by not making any 'sense' at all, the critic's role is a much
less 'inspired' one, and he is obligated, if he must persuade us, to
appeal to our reason, our common sense. But in view of some of
the statements contained in Addison Gayle's *The Black Aesthetic*,
there is reason to fear that we, as black critics, are beginning to
claim for ourselves the prerogatives of the artist. For, apart from
our probable fear of being charged with the ultimate crime of academic 'masturbation' and trivial 'mannerisms', it is difficult to explain away our apparent enthusiasms for the popular but mystifying phrase, the overly dogmatic assertion, the bombastic but
insupportable claim. James Emanuel identifies this danger in his
essay, and offers a timely warning against unreflecting judgment—

Being blindly black is preferable to being blindly white, in the
same way that becoming redemptively brave excels remaining

20

stubbornly secure; but neither attitude befits men whose ultimate mission is the salvation of a group larger than their own[17].

One can, however, see the point at which Professor Emanuel's sense of fair play leads him short of an unambiguous denunciation of the excessive idiosyncrasies of some of the critics he deals with. He ought, to be more precise, to have pointed out that Cecil Brown's strictures on Richard Wright are little better than palpable nonsense, and that Addison Gayle's interpretation of Baldwin's *Go Tell It on the Mountain* is at best an essay in intelligent distortion. Clearly, it would be futile to expect that the black critic, engaged in these momentous times in the reinterpretation of black literature is going to discharge his task without any presuppositions regarding this literature; to expect this would be to exhibit a stupendous lack of historical perspective, for it is precisely in respect of these presuppositions that the new concept of the Black Aesthetic may be thought to have significant value, to the extent, that is, that it seeks to prescribe certain broadly cultural stipulations as the necessary conditions of black art. But what, ironically, a good many of the proponents of this concept do not seem to recognise is this, that if theirs is a 'revolutionary' task, it is certainly less on account of their attempt to control the 'verbal image', even less because of any observable seriousness in their elucidation of already existing literature, but primarily because, unlike what may generally be termed the conservative Western approach to aesthetics, theirs is, not an ex post facto exercise, but a prescriptive, a priori one. One need hardly labour the point that, in general, 'Western' aesthetic theories, despite their occasional prescriptions, have been essentially analytic and descriptive, deriving their conclusions from the explication of already existing bodies of literature. The Black Aesthetic, on the other hand, is in essence a hypothetical one, a theory (or a body of theories) dealing with a yet unborn, though sometimes nascent art. Rather than limit itself to the task of deducing principles from what already exists as art, it seeks boldly to invoke its own definition of art into being, the result being that we are confronted with an exciting, if somewhat unusual situation, one in which criticism virtually

21

precedes art, its subject and reason for being. Despite its exciting elements, however, the situation in black criticism today would clearly have been a more healthy, and less meretricious one were many of our critics willing to admit not only that the evolution of novel principles is in itself a rewarding exercise but also that there does in fact exist a formidable body of black art that legitimately yields itself to useful analysis on the basis of a comprehensive aesthetic. Unfortunately, what we seem to have, instead, is a predominantly ahistorical and iconoclastic mood, in which there appears to be a pervasive and often inexplicable suspicion of our 'classic' black writers. It is, for instance, not at all easy to discover why William Kgotsitsile would wish to banish the Negritude poets from his pantheon of black artists, why Cecil Brown would want us to believe that Richard Wright was not really a black writer at all, or why Addison Gayle should argue that Ellison and Baldwin are men motivated in their art by the secret and incurable desire to become white. We deal in a little more detail with the question of historical continuities in Chapter Six, but it may be observed here that there is certainly a place for healthy scepticism in the evaluation of black writers, both past and present, but it is in our opinion equally clear that neither art nor its criticism is likely to gain from a capriciously ahistorical approach to black culture. We do not mean to imply by our reference to the historical sense that there are no valid distinctions to be made between writers like Senghor and LeRoi Jones, or between Gwendolyn Brooks and Don Lee; but we are not persuaded that these distinctions are any more significant than the equally valid similarities and links between these writers. Indeed there is, outrageous as this may sound, the ironic possibility that Jean Toomer's *Cane* validates the principles of the black aesthetic more plausibly than Jones' *The System of Dante's Hell* ever hopes to do, yet we are not aware that anyone would therefore conclude that Jean Toomer was 'blacker' than Jones is. And if this is true, it would seem that the black critic need not await the birth of a radically new body of literature nor dismiss out of hand the contributions of our older artists in order to grant validity to theories of the black aesthetic. In a culture whose contemporary mood appears often fundamentally to be an intensification of older, long-standing

22

intuitions, it appears to us so obvious, and yet so necessary to suggest that we are likely to abstract proof and justification for this aesthetic as much through examination of the works of McKay or James Weldon Johnson as through preoccupation with Edward Spriggs or Sonia Sanchez.

Prescriptions for a yet unborn art, if we do not regard them as absolute or immutable, do obviously have their advantages, particularly as they are involved with theoretical concepts regarding what black art *ought*, ideally, to be. James Emanuel may then be right when he concludes that, according to black artists, the ideal function of blackwriting '*should* be (emphasis ours) to build psychological peace within the black community while carrying on psychological war across the color line' [18]. Furthermore, though this is not too often admitted, futuristic prescription clearly has the advantage also of absolving the critic from the responsibility of coming positively to terms with what he already has as material for his endeavours, and thus Professor Gayle may, for instance, feel quite content with dispensing with the contributions of a man like Baldwin, and on a broader level, criticism becomes quite indistinguishable from an exercise in a chaotic form of creative inspiration.

The descriptive, or deductive approach to aesthetics has acquired respectability through the usage of many centuries, but it too does have its limitations, particularly since in dealing basically with already available material, the critic engaged in such a task is, in theory at any rate, wary of the kind of 'legislative' stipulation that makes the work of the prescriptive critic so much more exciting and innovative. But the deductive approach has the primary advantage of assuming a certain degree of historical continuity in the works available to the critic, and, what is perhaps even more important, he is certainly less prone to the temptation to banish large numbers of writers and their works from his range of concern. It need hardly be observed that as with apparent contradictions within a given culture, the varying and often conflicting perspectives of individual writers do sometimes constitute a higher pattern, and with respect to creative vision, it may be observed, for example, that William Melvin Kelley's approach to the issue of revolutionary action in the black community is an instinctual, visceral one in *A Different Drummer*, whereas John A. Williams' approach to the same issue in *The Man Who Cried I Am* is much more programmatic, more intellectual. Despite their varying approaches, the preoccupation of these two writers is so obviously identical that one can hardly be justified in limiting discussion of their achievement to the question as to which of them is closer to the spirit of the black aesthetic. We have deliberately simplified the matter in this manner in order to identify what we see as the misleading processes of thought that have led Professor Gayle, for instance, to the conclusion that in Baldwin's *Go Tell It on the Mountain*,

> . . . the tone of assimilation, the obsession with fusing the black and the white cultures—even at the risk of destroying the black —is . . . pervasive in the novel [19].

It is this type of criticism that we consider both limiting and undesirable, for not only does it fail to lend sufficient significance to historical continuities in black culture—the ecstasies and the psychic traumas of the religious life, for instance, which constitutes a major theme in this novel, is clearly not unrelated to the political passions of more recent black fiction—but it too glaringly also fails to recognise the quite ambitious manner in which Baldwin seeks in this novel to present an aesthetically valid vision of the black man's burden in America.

We discuss this novel in greater detail in Chapter Three, but it may be briefly observed here that fear, oppression, and the potentialities and failures of love are the three poles around which John Grimes' predicament revolves. His theological terror, his fear and hatred of God, is analogous to his fear and hatred of white society, and just as he seeks to transcend his fear of God through the power of his imagination, so also, with respect to political and social oppression, his only weapon (and this is worth bearing in mind in light of the often merely rhetorical rebellion in much later fiction) against white oppression appears to be his dream of vengeance. Furthermore, it ought to be observed that John hates and fears his earthly father with the same intensity with which he hates and fears God and white society. And if this is true, it becomes clear that

24

what we have in this novel is not the despicable attempt of a black boy to escape his condition by dreaming of whiteness, but the presentation of a powerful vision of his dilemma, a young man rendered impotent, except in his dreams, by the pervasiveness of this triadic threat to his existence. God, Gabriel, and the white man, with all they stand for, thus become for John both characters in themselves, and symbols of his fatal condition. With regard to the issue of historical realism, it seems to us that the view presented in this novel, the links, that is, between white oppression, religious fervour, and domestic feuds, is as close to what we know as reality as any other view one could think of. It may well be, then, that we have here a much more integrated and comprehensive vision of the black man's fate than we find in countless other novels. In terms of the black aesthetic, however, the major criticism that could be made against Baldwin's vision in this novel is certainly not that John is an assimilationist, but rather that the author appears to conceive of the possibility of triumph over his hero's fate as existing merely in the realm of imagination, rather than as a realisable alternative; but to recognise this limitation is surely not quite the same thing as dismissing the novel as being without value in the pantheon of black fiction.

It should be clear from the above that what we recommend is a critical approach that seeks not only to invoke a new art into being, but one also that recognises both the contributions and the limitations of the classic past. Indeed, as Professor Gayle would himself be willing to admit, the actualities, as distinct from the theories of the black aesthetic do in fact precede the very invention of the phrase, and if this is true, it would hardly seem intelligent to dismiss out of hand the contributions of such writers as Ellison, Baldwin and Wright to the evolution of the concept. The black critic is not likely to help matters if he wrote as though black literature began only ten years ago. Critical silence in the white establishment may be an ambiguous and perhaps ultimately irrelevant blessing, but a short-sighted view of history among black critics is to be wished for even less.

To the extent, therefore, that any 'principles' of criticism are directly applied in the following analysis of Baldwin's works, we may here briefly state that we proceed from three basic presuppositions: first, that he belongs, firmly and inseparably, to a continuous tradition in Black Literature in America; secondly, that we assume a necessary link between 'politics' and 'literature' and that what follows is therefore much closer to 'cultural' than to 'practical' criticism; and finally, that the concept of the black aesthetic is an eminently useful one that, bearing in mind the necessity for discriminations of quality and value, is as much applicable to Baldwin as to Don Lee.

Notes to Chapter One

1. Theodore Gross, 'Our Mutual Estate: The Literature of the American Negro,' in C. E. Bigsby, *The Black American Writer: Vol. 1, Fiction*, Florida, Everett Edwards, 1969, pp. 51–52
2. Consider, as an extremely urbane demonstration of this influence, Irving Howes 'radical' confusions in his references to LeRoi Jones in 'The Return of the Case of Ezra Pound,' *World*, Vol. 1, No. 9, Oct. 24, 1972, pp. 20–24
3. Harry Levin, 'Symbolism and Fiction,' in S. N. Grebstein, *Perspectives in Contemporary Criticism*, Harper and Row, 1968, p. 68
4. ibid., p. 69
5. Nathan Scott argues, on the contrary, that Wright's existentialist sympathies were quite natural for a man as dispossessed as he was. See Nathan Scott, 'The Dark and Haunted Tower of Richard Wright,' in Donald B. Gibson, ed., *Five Black Writers*, New York University Press, 1970, pp. 12–13
6. See the opening chapter in David Littlejohn, *Black On White: A Critical Survey of Writing by American Negroes*, Grossman, 1966
7. Mike Thelwell, 'Another Country: Baldwin's New York Novel,' in Bigsby, op.cit., p. 182
8. Richard Gilman, 'White Standards and Negro Writers,' in Bigsby, op.cit., p. 42
9. ibid.
10. John Henrik Clarke, ed., *William Styron's Nat Turner: Ten Black Writers Respond*, Beacon Press, 1969
11. See David Lewis, *King: A Critical Biography*, Praeger, 1970, p. 258 ff
12. John A. Williams, *The King God Didn't Save*, Coward-McCann, 1970
13. John A. Williams, *The Man Who Cried I Am*, Signet, 1967, pp. 323–24
14. Williams, *The King God Didn't Save*, p. 217
15. William Kgotsitsile, 'Paths to the Future,' in Addison Gayle, ed., *The Black Aesthetic*, Doubleday, 1971, pp. 257–58

16. See, e.g., V. Nabokov's comments in *New York Review of Books*, Oct. 7, 1971, p. 413
17. James A. Emanuel, in Gayle, op.cit., p. 218
18. ibid. p. 209
19. Gayle, op.cit., p. 413

Two

'The Amen Corner'

James Baldwin's continuous attempts to come to terms with his inheritance in the Western world have earned him a certain genteel notoriety in the history of American letters. The passionately apocalyptic vision, the pained discomfiture in the realm of morals, the evangelistic fervour and the biblical rhetoric are elements in his writings that ultimately derive from his long apprenticeship and briefer ministry in the Black Church in Harlem. From a more technical perspective, also, the extent to which he has so far shown an ability to control the fictional form is clearly not unrelated to the rhetorical practices of the Black Ministry; but beyond the generalized and now somewhat mandatory notices that have been made between the mood of his writings and his personal history, little serious attempt has so far been made to identify the precise manner in which his religious background has been for him both a source of creative inspiration and of conceptual and psychological constraint.

Students of the history of the Black Church in America are agreed that the practice of Black Christianity has always been ambiguous in its objectives; they will admit that while its joyless rejection of the things of the world in favour of a hypothetical paradise was more akin to the dreams of the early Christians, its very faith in the possibility of another, better world was in itself a subjective response to the actual condition of its members. While, that is, the rhetoric of the city of God may have been a somewhat impractical indulgence, the very mythology of Black Christianity, with its curiously appropriate analogies to the biblical accounts of the Jewish exile, may also be seen as a strategy of guarded political protest.

For those who are overwhelmed by the often fatal inequities of their social condition, there is an understandable temptation to reject the real world as evil, and this rejection is often accompanied by a feverish anticipation of the millennial Eden, of an age in which there shall be neither pain nor injustice.

"To a people without circumstantial hope", Reuben Sheres has written, "(the Black Church) offered the hope of the by and by . . . The circumstances of the existing world were bad enough that (sic) they needed to be denied or rejected . . . and in their place was substituted the hope of the world to come" [1].

The oppressed, it is true, cannot make any exclusive claims to the knowledge of evil, but it is also true that when understood as much in its social as in its metaphysical meaning, evil is a reality with which they are only too familiar. That the congregations of the Black Church should thus have been preoccupied with the celestial city is, therefore, quite understandable, but it should also be emphasized that its millennialism was, almost by definition, equally a strategy of protest, an expression of dissatisfaction with the real condition of the members of these congregations. Indeed, the very transformation of the Church from an 'invisible institution' to an established and transparently Black organization was, in itself, an act of moderate defiance, a gesture of denunciation of the inhumanity of the older, white churches; and the long line of ministers and preachers who, through the history of this church have seen and taken advantage of the possibilities of social leadership offered by it is, clearly, an indication of its political significance.

Nevertheless, despite the implication of 'protest' that is involved in any definition of utopianism, religious or political, it must be observed that the true strength of the Black Church lay rather in the power of its metaphorical evocations than in any actual confrontations it may have had with white oppression. Lawrence Jones' observations in this regard are no doubt well-meaning enough, but he rather strains credibility when he claims that

. . . viewed through the prism of present rhetoric, it becomes clear that one of the issues being contested in the founding of the Black Churches was Black Power [2].

The Black minister, it is true, occasionally managed to acquire a measure of actual political influence in proportion to the size of his congregation, as shown by the more recent example of Martin Luther King's meteoric career; but in general, political protest in the Black Church was a matter of analogical references to biblical history. The generic white man was Pharaoh, from whose oppression a black Moses was some day to arise to rescue his brethren, and America was Egypt, the land of sin and evil and godlessness that was doomed to suffer the brunt of God's fiery vengeance[3]. There were compelling practical reasons for this preference for indirect imagery. The certainty of furious reprisals, of the white back-lash, ensured that the 'protest' of the Black Church should be couched in such terms as to render it lame and largely unavailing[4]. And in a world in which terror and suffering were more real than the possibility of ideal justice in society, the feverish anticipation of bliss in heaven became a more rewarding exercise than any attempt to confront the evil in the actual world.

The millennialism and the metaphorical protest in Black Christianity are two major elements that were later to be dramatized in Baldwin's writings, but there was a third element which, in our opinion, is even more significant for an understanding of Baldwin's career so far. We have seen how, in response to the actual suffering of its members, the Black Church evolved a theology in which the promise of the celestial city took on a lurid fascination for them, and we have suggested that practical considerations of safety contributed to the rhetorical extravagances of this theology. For the preacher who contemplated the plight of his congregation, safety, the evasion or assuagement of white anger, lay in metaphor, in indirect statement. He could offer them citizenship in heaven, and he could inveigh against the corruption of Sodom and Gomorrah, against the oppression of the Pharaohs with far more impunity than he could decry, in straightforward language, their real suffering. But he knew also, with a chill puritan certainty, that not all his flock would automatically gain entrance into heaven. Promising them the city of God, he also reminded them of the visitation of God's anger on all who chose the path of evil and sin. And since he knew how much more accessible the path of damnation was, his predictions of doom were even more passionate than his promises of divine intervention. And so he left in the minds of his congregation an indelible fear, a vision of their corruption, of the dangers they courted if they were ensnared by the temptations of the white man's world.

Such was the theology of Baldwin's adolescence in America. Everywhere he turned he saw the manifestations of sin. The Harlem of his boyhood was, and still is, as close to an illustration of the contours of hell as could be found anywhere in the real world. At home, his father was a discontented, imperious patriarch whose single-minded religious fervour was as formidable as his permanent rage; at school and on the streets, he saw only omens of his own personal corruptibility[5]. Under such conditions, it was not inevitable that Baldwin should see the social horror around him primarily as a paradigm of metaphysical evil; but given the pervading squalor, both of spirit and of environment that he saw around him, it is perhaps understandable that he should have felt he had no right to expect to be spared the fate of his friends and playmates. At fourteen he entered the church in search of safety, having convinced himself that safety was 'synonymous with God'. Four years later he was out of the church; it had given him little more than the illusion of safety, and it had sought to curtail both his freedom of action and of imagination. It was at this time that he took the curiously not unrelated decision of becoming a writer.

The practice of Black Christianity, we have argued, was in part a strategy of escape, and in so far as its anticipation of the millennium encouraged in many of its members a certain suspicion of all practical involvement in life, the innocence that they sought to defend, their feeling of safety, was obviously illusory. But the illusion of safety, given the proper intensity of imagination, can be just as palpable as the real thing, so that despite its often joyless denials of the fullness of life, the Black Church did serve a quite tangible role in the life of its members. It gave them a refuge, a rallying point around which they sought to lessen their pain by sharing in one another's joys and suffering. It offered them a brotherhood of the dispossessed which they could not find anywhere else. Yet despite this essential role it also engendered in the minds of its members a curious psychic condition that may properly be termed cosmic terror. In addition to the brief spells of ecstasy granted them in their visions of the celestial life, they were also made intensely aware of the agonies of damnation. They dreamed of heaven, but were persuaded they could be certain of their candidacy for hell. They hoped to be numbered among the saints, but knew more about the devil and his snares. This Manichean cleavage in Black theology was by no means unique—it had perfectly respectable historical antecedents in America—but the more directly socio-political sources of this cleavage gave it a measure of pertinent immediacy that was lacking in the imagination of the Puritans.

The millennialism, the apocryphal imagination, the equation of metaphorical plaintiveness with actual political rage are, then, elements in Baldwin's writings that derive from the period of his involvement with the church in Harlem. But to understand more fully the nature of his long and painful conceptual journey from the time of the publication of *Go Tell It on the Mountain* to that of *No Name in the Street* it is necessary to emphasize the role that 'theological terror' has played as a dynamic in this development. Ralph Ellison has argued, in reference to the Blues, that they are motivated by an impulse

. . . to keep the painful details and episodes of a brutal experience alive in one's aching consciousness, to finger its ragged grain, and to transcend it, not by the consolation of philosophy, but by squeezing from it a near-tragic, near-comic lyricism[6].

Baldwin will probably deny that there was anything 'near-comic' in his personal experience, but he might agree that one way to triumph over terror is constantly to return to the scene of one's brutalization, if, that is, one survives. Terror was, for him, an essential factor in his adolescence. "I became, during my fourteenth year", he has written, "afraid—afraid of the evil within me and afraid of the evil without" [7]. Both at home and on the streets, he was constantly reminded of his own sinfulness, of the abyss of corruption that waited to engulf him. And it was not merely his fear of being arrested or brutalized by the ubiquitous police, nor of joining the hordes of pimps and racketeers, dope-addicts and criminals around him. His fear was much more harrowing, much more quintessential; it was a cosmic dread, a terror of life itself. And since he felt that his period in the church had been something in the nature of a perfectly luxurious dalliance, the only choice left him was to transform his fears, by constantly returning to them, into a tragic lyricism.

"I've always been afraid", he was later to observe, "but I was lucky . . . Because if you're frightened enough, there's nothing to be frightened of. So you just have to keep moving, because, if you don't, if your fear is great enough, you'll just simply . . . perish" [8].

To 'keep moving' has been for Baldwin a constant revisiting of the sources of his dread, so that what, if inexpertly handled, could be a merely morbid fascination with 'the dark night of the soul' has become in Baldwin's hands a crucial and lyric struggle to save himself from spiritual chaos. He does not, to be sure, always succeed in bridging the gap between sheer morbid obsession and the artistic tenderness necessary to convert this into a serious statement of an existential dilemma. In *Go Tell It on the Mountain*, for example, the character of Gabriel, in all his profound egotism and primeval grandeur, is drawn with a sure hand, with a measure of compassion that makes him a truly imposing figure, whereas, in *Giovanni's Room*, there is a kind of tortured ambiguity in the presentation of David that turns this novel into a statement of unconvincing heresy. We do not mean to suggest that his more public stance, as political and moral rebel, is any less important to an understanding of his achievement; but we do, as we shall later illustrate, argue that it is precisely because his earliest concern had been to come to terms with a private, rather than a public predicament that he demonstrated a political naivety in his earlier writings that was sometimes quite amazing.

Baldwin's heritage was, then, twofold. There was the heritage of fear, which was to lead to the intensely moral admonitions of his earlier writings, and there was the heritage of veiled anger, which was later to be converted into a quintessential social fury in his more recent works. For, just as the political implications in the practice of Black Christianity were never entirely invalidated by its more utopian concerns, so also it would be futile to seek to separate the political from the more metaphysical perspective of Baldwin's performance. We seek therefore not to establish the workings of a dissociated sensibility but the record of a writer whose major, though not exclusive, preoccupation was for a long time less the need to express political rage than the compulsion to come to terms with a private nightmare. And in this regard it is instructive to consider Baldwin's objections to *Uncle Tom's Cabin*, Harriet Beecher Stowe's famous contribution to American social protest fiction.

When 'Everybody's Protest Novel' appeared in Partisan Review in 1949, the yardstick of critical responses to writings by black Americans was Richard Wright's *Native Son*, published in 1940. Those black writers who chose to write in the manner of Wright's furious rage and social determinisms were likely to be dismissed as pamphleteers and propagandists, and those who chose to conceal their alienation and rage were more likely to be received as promising artists. The fifties were, as everyone knows, the period when the critical establishment was tired and wary of confrontations. It was the time when it was fashionable to couch legitimate despair in the elegant existentialist rhetoric of Camus, a time when disillusionment over the meaningfulness of 'causes' led to often sophistical explorations of the personal psyche. Many black writers practising at the time were not immune to this spirit of the age. Ironically, Richard Wright, who had himself been largely instrumental in forcing the issue of social injustice upon the consciousness of American critics, was to publish, in 1953, *The Outsider*—a novel in which the existentialist fad which had always been there in Wright's vision is perhaps inordinately pronounced. Ralph Ellison was also to publish in this decade his single novel, *Invisible Man*, in which his hero's sense of commitment to a cause is underscored by a compulsive desire finally to justify his own personal existence. It seems useful to bear this in mind as a necessary perspective on the significance of Baldwin's critical attitudes at this time. He had, in 1949, hardly established himself even as a candidate for impor-

35

tance in the American Pantheon and, confronted with what appeared to him to be the formidable standards already laid down by Wright, he may have felt the need to strike out on his own (an illusory feeling, clearly, since it was in fact to become the standard mood of the fifties) to establish a different perspective from which he hoped to be judged. His quarrel with Wright was, in a sense, a classic instance of the younger writer's desire to destroy his older mentor's hold over him before he could start out on his own. If we must believe Baldwin's own later apologies, the issue of protest must have been a crucial one in his quarrel with Wright[9], but since it is itself a largely academic issue, one may suppose that Baldwin probably felt a stronger, if unconscious, need simply to take an individual stand. In any case, his magisterial pronouncements on both Wright and Mrs. Stowe had all the makings of a *cause célèbre,* and the sheer drama of this rather one-sided confrontation appears to have led many to believe that he had made a significant contribution to the refutation of the literature of protest.

Obviously, there is a sense in which one can say that this essay was partly aimed at re-establishing the aesthetic primacy of art, partly an indication of Baldwin's own vexation over the constraints upon the writer's freedom imposed by the superficial need to interpret man and his life as though he were significant merely in communion with other men. Perhaps, too, this vexation was a healthy token of his own commitment to art, a welcome theoretical counterpoise to the temptation toward unselective naturalism. Nevertheless the implications of this commitment, especially for the black writer, were only part of a dual responsibility which Baldwin inevitably assumed when he chose to become a writer. He was *expected* to demonstrate a certain competence in dealing artistically with the raw material of his experience, but it was also assumed that since the nature of this experience was a peculiar one, there were necessary conclusions to be drawn from such peculiarity. In other words, rather than see the black writer as burdened by a dilemma of contradictions, it is more useful to see his aesthetic and 'political' responsibilities as constituting a pattern of related obligations that negate neither the meaning of his experience nor his desire to express this in an artistically satisfying way. And if it is admitted that this assumed conflict of obligations is indeed no more than a pattern of complementary functions which Baldwin must himself have recognised, it becomes clear that we should read 'Everybody's Protest Novel' not as an indispensable refutation of protest fiction, which it quite obviously is not, but as an essay whose primary concerns were of far more personal significance to Baldwin.

The essay deals with what Baldwin sees as the two major perspectives in *Uncle Tom's Cabin*—the political and the theological—and his identification of the latter perspective is, in our opinion, a useful index to his own preoccupations at the time. *Uncle Tom's Cabin*, despite its obvious inadequacies as a work of art, was acclaimed as having helped dramatize the issues involved in the controversy over slavery, and it was generally assumed that its concerns were more political and ethical than theological. It was generally thought, too, that Mrs. Stowe's own religious convictions had a good deal to do with the conclusions she reached in this novel, and it is these convictions that Baldwin chooses to question in his essay, though he gets down to this via a rather superficial discussion of protest fiction in general.

He is quite unambiguous in his dismissal of this novel. *"Uncle Tom's Cabin"*, he bluntly states, "is a very bad novel", and few will quarrel with this cryptic dismissal. "It is", he explains, "ridden with virtuous sentimentality", with "the ostentatious parading of excessive and spurious emotion" [10], the result, he goes on to add, of a fundamental dishonesty. There is, he argues, something unduly specious about Mrs. Stowe's virtuous outrage, a glibness that is the outcome of superficial feeling, an indication of a deeper aridity of emotion. And because such a merely putative moral outrage does not come from true feeling, Baldwin assures us in vigorous rhetoric that her declamations are merely "the signal of secret and violent inhumanity, the mark of cruelty" [11].

Moving from the excessive sentimentality of this novel, he goes on to identify what he sees as the motiveless brutality, the senseless and irrational violence that are, again, the signal of a basic lack of concern in Mrs. Stowe's vision. He considers, for a brief moment, the possibility that the defects of this novel are more the mark of technical incompetence than of a lack of moral integrity, but quickly moves from so charitable a concession to a rather lurid discussion of the limitations of protest literature in general. Protest literature, he argues, is false because it seeks to deny man's freedom; man is not merely a member of a group or community, he is not to be explained away merely as Aristotle's political beast, nor by the quasi-profundities of scientific jargon. Rather (and here one suspects that Baldwin gets carried away by his rhetoric) man is

. . . something more than that, something resolutely indefinable, unpredictable. In overlooking, denying, evading his complexity—which is nothing more than the disquieting complexity of ourselves—we are diminished and we perish; only within this web of ambiguity, paradox, this hunger, danger, darkness, can we find at once ourselves and the power that will free us from ourselves[12].

These failures, then, Baldwin argues, the murky sentimentality, the motiveless brutality, the temptation to adopt the facile explanation of man as a social being devoid of all paradox and complexity, these are faults attributable not so much to Mrs. Stowe's incompetence as a novelist as to her fundamental aridity of heart, to a failure of sensibility in her.

Yet despite his forcefully expressed vexation with Mrs. Stowe's attempts to politicize man, it further appears that Baldwin is in this essay even more fascinated with what he sees as her less than heroic struggle with metaphysical evil. Her morality, he argues, is a medieval one—she conceives of her soul as suspended between heaven and the flames of hell—she has an unduly morbid sense of her own sinfulness, and is therefore inclined to see political immorality in ultimately theological terms. And because slavery is politically unethical, she is obsessed by a sense of communal guilt. Since damnation is the reward for unexpiated sin, Mrs. Stowe, Baldwin argues, is driven toward a ritual of expiation, hence her feverish attempt to transform Uncle Tom, her hero, into an emasculated, dehumanized black man[13]. Uncle Tom, then, is the sacrificial beast, the symbol of her attempts to bargain for her salvation, the manifestation of her fear and her desire for grace. The novel, he concludes,

> . . . is activated by what might be called a theological terror, the terror of damnation; and the spirit that breathes in this book, hot, self-righteous, fearful, is not different from that spirit of medieval times which sought to exorcise evil by burning witches[14].

Here we see, then, plausible enough evidence to suggest that Baldwin's preoccupations in this essay are not so much to identify the limitations of protest fiction as to emphasize what he sees as the basically theological motives that engendered this novel. The validity of his views, with regard to Mrs. Stowe's motives, is, of course, open to question, and ultimately it may not be of much significance whether she was driven by a passion for justice in society or by the desire to earn herself a place in heaven—the two are, in fact, not necessarily exclusive of each other as motivations. But if we are not interested in Mrs. Stowe's motives, we are certainly concerned to discover why Baldwin is less preoccupied with the political implications of her novel than with her theological superstitions; and since criticism is as much a reflection of a given critical imagination as it is of the object of critical concern, it is plausible to argue that Baldwin's response to *Uncle Tom's Cabin* was predetermined by an apocalyptic vision arising from his own personal religious experience and bearing a close resemblance to the 'theological terror' which he sought to identify in this novel. We hope to show—by a brief analysis of *The Fire Next Time*, Baldwin's own famous contribution to the dramatization of political issues—that the initial, and perhaps abiding dynamic in Baldwin's imagination has been the same 'theological terror', the same despair, the same dread of hell.

If 'Everybody's Protest Novel' was wrongly received as a useful refutation of the validity of protest fiction, the response to *The Fire Next Time* was appreciably more complex though, in the main, no less misconceived. In general, it was recognised that whatever social analysis there was in this latter essay was tantamount to a condemnation of American mores, and that the passion of Baldwin's prophecies boded ill for American civilization. The essay was justly seen as the mark of a talent fast approaching stylistic maturity, and in accordance with that peculiarly American tendency to equate self-criticism with moral health, there appears now to have been a somewhat morbid fascination with the forcefulness of his denunciations, with the awesomeness of his predictions. It was not that many did not feel blackmailed by his prophecy, but, it was generally felt that since anger objectified was anger mediated, the fact that so talented a spokesman for the oppressed could speak with such directness and so fearlessly (after all the fury of his essay was far removed from the tepid, veiled displeasures of the black Ministers of long ago) could not but augur well for America's claim to being a democratic republic. There was obviously a good deal of fantasy, of deliberate self-hypnosis in all this, though it is also true that Baldwin's own ambiguities encouraged these delusions. Nevertheless, it cannot be overstated that in thus emphasizing the public and overtly social implications of this study, we were probably guilty of doing Baldwin a great injustice, precisely by failing to recognise the private hell from which he cried, his primarily theological preoccupations in this essay. 'The fire next time' was for him less a metaphor for potential social chaos than a realistically imagined prophecy of apocalyptic damnation. For him the truly terrible consequence of social injustice was not revolution, not a violent disruption of the social order, but quite literally, fire and brimstone—the burning in hell of the guilty soul. In other words, Baldwin's idea of man was at the time neither Aristotelian nor even existential, and certainly nothing as uncomplicated as the Marxist theory of society implies. The ideal society was for him not one in which 'civil rights' were assured to all, nor one in which justice and freedom prevailed, but that society in which man is absolved from the threat and the burden of damnation—a society in which he is assured of salvation. Thus, while such words as 'freedom', 'justice' and 'love' appear quite frequently in the pages of this essay, we are required to understand them not in their 'infantile American sense', in their secular implications, but as attempts to describe a higher, other-worldly reality.

One source of the misconceptions that attended this essay is the fact that Baldwin begins with a very moving and detailed account of what it meant to grow up in Harlem; and because there is in this account that element of graphic and deeply felt realism that moves us either to pity or rage, we are tempted to conclude that the writer's objective is the search for political solutions. And indeed, on a superficial level of comprehension the logical conclusion to the social analysis in this essay is a political, even a revolutionary one— an implicit call for forceful confrontation. There is a burning need to put an end to the sufferings of black people in America; one should expect to be able to persuade white people, through reasoning, of this necessity; but experience shows that it is futile to expect them to act decisively out of their own convictions, since it is against their interest to do so. Therefore, black people have no choice but to adopt more radical methods. He concludes:

> There is simply no possibility of a real change in the Negro's situation without the most radical and far-reaching changes in the American political and social structure[15].

And if it is objected that this call to action lacks in clarity, Baldwin, a few pages later, makes it quite clear what he has in mind:

> At the center of this dreadful storm, this vast confusion, stand the black people of this nation, who must now share the fate of a nation that has never accepted them, to which they were brought in chains. Well, if this is so, one has no choice but to do all in one's power to change that fate, and at no matter what risk— eviction, imprisonment, torture, death[16].

There is in these passages an implicit political imperative that carries with it the potential, at least, of violent confrontation, and if this is so, it becomes clear that the logical solutions which Baldwin has to offer here are curiously not unlike the 'whatever means necessary' policy of more radical black groups in this country. And only in this limited sense can one regard this essay as one in which there is a logical link between analysis and conclusion, between angry denunciations and the counsels of mitigation offered.

But the ultimate conclusion of this essay is, in essence, a world

41

removed from so logical and uncomplicated a choice as the political imperative here identified; there appears to be for Baldwin something so specious and inadequate in such a choice that, more unconsciously than deliberately, he shies away from it and finally elects to bear witness to a transcendental reality that appears to us to have precious little to do with our ugly lives. And because he has never, until very recently, felt comfortable with the political definition of man, he sets out to propose an alternative definition that for all its testimony to Baldwin's high moral rectitude nevertheless strikes us as being elegantly impractical. Observe, for example, his prescription of love: a people as incapable as Americans are of comprehending the meaning and responsibilities of love are doomed, and "I use the word love", he cautions, "here not merely in the personal sense but as a state of being, or a state of grace— not in the infantile American sense of being made happy but in the tough and universal sense of quest and daring and growth" [17]. "Freedom", he further asserts in this transcendental construct, is no longer primarily a concept to be understood in terms of sociopolitical relationships, but a spiritual attribute that comes only to those who have attained it through constant striving. He contends:

I have met only a few people—and most of them were not Americans, who had any real desire to be free. Freedom is hard to bear. It can be objected that I am speaking of political freedom in spiritual terms, but the political institutions of any nation are always menaced and ultimately controlled by the spiritual state of that nation [18].

And finally, in like manner, his conception of suffering is here not primarily limited to its negative implication of painful deprivation, but expanded to embrace what appears to us to be a curiously masochistic indulgence. He declares:

I do not mean to be sentimental about suffering, but people who cannot suffer can never grow up, can never discover who they are. That man who is forced each day to snatch his manhood, his identity, out of the fire of human cruelty that rages to destroy it

42

knows, if he survives his effort, and even if he does not survive it, something about himself and human life that no school on earth —and, indeed, no church—can teach [19].

There is something touchingly lyrical about Baldwin's moral consolations here, and as a prescription for the ideal existence his interpretation of life can, to be sure, hardly be faulted, since it derives its validity from the best in Christian idealism. There is, too, doubtless a level of apprehension in which such impeccable and universally applicable axioms may indeed be said to constitute the very distinction of this essay. Nevertheless, it is conceivable that there are many who will find Baldwin's stoic transcendentalisms somewhat unrealistic, or even downright dishonest[20]. We need not, however, be particularly concerned with the validity of his recommendations. It is ultimately irrelevant for our purposes here whether or not we agree with him that personal virtue is the key to social justice, whether or not it is true that such proprieties of thought as he demonstrates here presuppose a certain deliberate act of detachment from harsh realities. We need only identify the curious dichotomy between the graphic realism of his social analysis and the extravagance of his transcendental conclusions, and attempt to offer some explanation for this state of affairs.

We began by identifying those aspects of Black Christianity which appear, in retrospect, to have profoundly influenced Baldwin's vision of life, and we have argued that given the intensely individualized dread of hell that was part of the theology of black inspirational worship, it is understandable that Baldwin's imagination should have taken, initially at any rate, this 'theological terror' as the *terminus a quo* of his concern with the riddle of life. We have also tried to show how, in his comments on *Uncle Tom's Cabin*, this terror led him to conclusions regarding this novel that appeared finally to have little to do with the socio-political conditions that primarily motivated Mrs. Stowe's novel. In the case of *The Fire Next Time*, it seems plausible to argue that the same essential dynamic is at work. Baldwin's fear in this essay is not the fear of the consequences of violent revolution; the doom he foresees is not to be understood in merely secular terms. Like the preacher that he once was, his obsessive concern here is with the fate of the soul, and with his preacher's consciousness he addresses the American polity as he would his congregation, admonishing, blackmailing, threatening, but just as the effectiveness of the preacher's sermon depended on the extent to which he himself believed in the apocalyptic vision he sought to impress his flock with, so also the credibility of Baldwin's prophecies of disaster derives from his own passionate belief in its certainty. And so it turns out that if Mrs. Stowe's novel is indeed motivated by her theological terror, the mood of Baldwin's own essay is dictated also by an equally intense fear of damnation, a fear that led to the curious inconsistencies we have tried to identify in *The Fire Next Time*. But to say that there is a certain similarity between the terror in *Uncle Tom's Cabin* and Baldwin's own fear of damnation is of course to make a sweeping generalization that needs qualification. If it is true, as he insists, that the essential motivation in the former novel is the quest for grace, the same cannot properly be said to be true of his own writings, for the distinction between Mrs. Stowe's novel and Baldwin's own works is the precise distinction between the ritual of expiation and ritual heresy. Put differently, it is the difference which he himself sees between 'defending' oneself against one's fears and facing these fears. "To defend oneself against a fear", he declares in *The Fire Next Time*, "is to ensure that one will, one day, be conquered by it; fears must be faced" [21]. And we must be careful here to understand the precise use of this terminology. To defend oneself against a fear is ultimately unavailing, precisely because the mechanisms employed in fact imply an unconscious admission of the power that one's fears have over one. To face a fear, on the other hand, painful though this may be, is an indication of an at least putative refusal to admit its power. Thus, when Mrs. Stowe, in her quest for salvation and her dread of the symbolic power of blackness transforms Uncle Tom into an impotent cipher of a man, she nonetheless remains the permanent victim of her dread because she still believes in the demonic power of blackness; whereas when Baldwin, in *Go Tell It on the Mountain*, gives us an account of a young man's turbulent adolescence in which intimations of profane love, in the extreme form of homosexuality, are structurally integrated into the drama of a seemingly devout conversion, we are expected to understand that this profanity, this heresy, is in itself an act of defiance against God. In both cases, however, it seems clear that it is not in the absence of a tormented vision of hell that we shall find the precise uses to which ritual has been put. Both in the instance of what Baldwin would have us accept is a more unquestioning belief in the reality of hell in Harriet Stowe's imagination, and in his own more tortuous and complex defiance of this power, what we finally have are two sensibilities curiously attracted to each other, for whom private visions of hell and damnation are apparently more real than issues of more public consequence, and it is in the identification of this fascination with the tragic potentiality of *'homo theologicus'* that we shall find the true meaning of Baldwin's struggle to achieve an authentic voice.

Baldwin's tendency to interpret man rather as a theological than as a political animal has served him often and well as a source of lyric inspiration, but it has also been an obstacle in his progress toward conceptual maturity. For, while this theological view of man, when it was properly employed in his art, as in *Go Tell It on the Mountain*, provided a meaningful dramatic conflict that made this novel so eminently readable, he must have understood that in deciding to become a writer, and his theoretical presuppositions notwithstanding, he was taking upon himself a perhaps terrible, and certainly irksome responsibility. For, if to be a good writer is in itself a difficult enough task, to be a good *black* writer in an age of dramatic confrontations is an even more impossible avocation— one in which the development of a meaningful public voice is as indispensable as the formulation of a private vision of life. And we do not here mean to make any unduly precious claims for the black writer. It is perfectly conceivable that Baldwin could still have achieved respectable fame as a writer merely by employing his sense of private dread as absolute and permanent theme, especially as the sources of this dread were so closely interwoven into his social experience. But it must also be admitted that to conceive of man's fate exclusively in terms of his individual predicament, or even in terms alone of his spiritual existence is, if not specious, certainly constricting, especially for a writer who appeared to be so concerned to celebrate the amplitude of man's life. And if this is so, we may then expect that the black writer will achieve a mature and unified vision only when, despite the immediacy of his own private nightmare, he has learned how, in his art, to superimpose on his own suffering an awareness that it is not unique, but part of a social dilemma that many more like him have to contend with. Thus, then, we may legitimately expect that Baldwin's struggle with theological terror, his attempts to exorcise, to destroy the sources of his apocalyptic dread, are initial steps in his progress toward the achievement of a more public voice, and we may further expect this progress to be demonstrated in his writings. It will be our task to show that this is the case, but the journey toward maturity has not been without turbulence and false steps. Any reader of Baldwin's fictions will no doubt admit that there is in his works a chronological spiral of rage, that in terms of degrees of anger, *Another Country* is obviously more searing and lethal than *Go Tell It on the Mountain*, and that in a very fundamental sense, the rage in *Tell Me How Long the Train's Been Gone* and in *No Name in the Street* is both of a different category and also much more terrifying in its implications. But intensity of rage cannot in itself be seen as an effective gauge of growing maturity; rather, it is the extent to which this rage is integrated within a structurally plausible creative vision that we must search for indications of growth. In the case of Baldwin, it is probable that the relation between rage and structural plausibility has been a parasitic one, the rage feeding, apparently, on his sense of structural unity, and it would be rewarding to inquire into the details of this parasitic condition in his works.

Notes to Chapter Two

1. Reuben Sheares, 'Beyond White Theology', in *Christianity and Crisis: A Journal of Christian Opinion*, Vol. XXX, No. 18 (Nov. 2 & 16, 1970), p. 231
2. Lawrence Jones, 'Black Churches in Historical perspective', op.cit., p. 228

3. An examination of the Spirituals, a somewhat litanical expression of the typical minister's sermons, should illustrate this point. On the controversy over the meaning of the Spirituals, see E. Franklin Frazier, *The Negro Church in America*, Schocken, 1963, p. 12, and James Cone, *Black Theology and Black Power*, p. 105

4. Edward Margolies, *Native Sons: A Critical Study of Twentieth Century Negro American Authors*, J. B. Lippincott, 1969, pp. 103–104

5. James Baldwin, *The Fire Next Time*, Dell, 1964, p. 27 ff

6. Ralph Ellison, 'Richard Wright's Blues', in *Shadow and Act*, Signet, 1966, p. 90

7. Baldwin, *The Fire Next Time*, p. 28

8. Baldwin, cited in Fern Marja Eckman, *The Furious Passage of James Baldwin*, M. Evans, 1966, p. 98

9. Baldwin, 'Alas Poor Richard', in *Nobody Knows My Name*, London, Corgi, 1965, p. 146 ff

10. Baldwin, 'Everybody's Protest Novel', in *Notes of a Native Son*, Bantam, 1964, p. 10

11. ibid.

12. ibid., p. 11

13. ibid., pp. 12–13

14. ibid., p. 13

15. Baldwin, *The Fire Next Time*, p. 115

16. ibid., p. 139

17. ibid., p. 128

18. ibid., p. 120

19. ibid., pp. 132–33

20. See, e.g., John Illo, 'The Rhetoric of Malcolm X', in Peter Spackman, ed., *Columbia University Forum Anthology*, IX, iii (1966), p. 260

21. Baldwin, *The Fire Next Time*, p. 42

Three

Baldwin's Quarrel with God

It was Lionel Trilling who, in 1963, cautioned us against the tendency to think of Wordsworth mainly as the poet who defined poetry as the spontaneous overflow of powerful feelings or as emotion recollected in tranquility[1]. In the context of Black literature in this country, it was a timely and salutary reminder that such easy explanations could be quite misleading if not adequately qualified. The decade of the Sixties was both the decade of Black rage and of the flowering of Baldwin's talent, and particularly after the publication of *Another Country*, there was a general tendency to employ the argument from anger as both justification and permanent dynamic in the latter's writings. But Baldwin's beginnings were nothing so simple. The desperate months in Europe when he laboured with *Go Tell It on the Moutain* were certainly not memorable for their tranquility, nor was the labour of gestation itself a particularly spontaneous one. Rather, the novel was the result of almost ten years of false starts, shattered hopes and numbing frustrations, and we must therefore look elsewhere for the sources and origins of this important novel.

In a certain sense, his beginnings as a writer were quite typical. He actively participated in the production of his High School newspaper, some of his teachers willingly recognised his promise, and he himself had quite made up his mind, by the time he was sixteen, that he was going to become an important writer. By 1944 when he had his first crucial meeting with Richard Wright, he had been writing for some time, and had in fact produced the first sixty pages of his first abortive novel, a fact which was the main justification for his meeting with Wright. And for those who are inclined to see

49

political rage as the primary motivation in Baldwin's writings, it is instructive to recall the reasons why this novel was never published. Richard Wright was, in the forties, the major literary light in the black community, and a good many of the young black writers who began their careers during this period felt in some way pressed to follow his example and write in accordance with the standards he had set, especially in *Native Son*. Baldwin was later to discover, and to announce his discovery in a quite spectacular manner, that admiration for an older writer did not necessarily imply the obligation to indiscriminately imitate him. He was not, he later contended, about to become another Richard Wright, and his early efforts at writing had proved unsuccessful because he had listened to too many advisers who expected only a certain kind of writing from black writers.

It was not unusual that Baldwin should have failed to get his first novel accepted for publication, and as he himself was later to admit, this early failure did give him the opportunity of reassessing his own objectives and of discovering his abilities and limitations. He could not be another Richard Wright precisely because the sources of his discontent were fundamentally different from Wright's. Where Wright was driven to write by a *political* rage of uncomplicated intensity, Baldwin brought to his ambition of becoming a writer an intricate web of psychological complexes that were distinguished more by fear than by anger. If the urge to express his rage against social oppression was for Wright the primary necessity, Baldwin could not arrive at this stage without destroying, first, his theological dread, his sense of personal corruption, and his fear of his father. To begin, as he had tried, and as he had been advised to do, by dealing with the public aspects of his alienation, was inevitably to court failure, since such a start seemed to presuppose that the sources of the individual talent were identical in all respects, in all writers of the same colour; and it was of crucial importance that he should discover this false assumption at the very beginning of his career. Six months after the failure of his first novel, he gave eloquent notice of his discovery in 'Everybody's Protest Novel', and if the sentiments expressed in this essay could hardly be accepted as a permanent or definitive refutation of the literature of social protest, it had the more limited value of indicating the direction in which his more immediate preoccupations were likely to lead him.

Baldwin's dilemma was threefold. By the time *Go Tell* was ready for publication, he had formally broken away from the Church in Harlem, but this formal renunciation of the ministry was by no means a reliable indication that he had truly won that freedom from the terror of sin which the break was meant to imply. He was indeed by 1954 no longer a member of any church, but the habits of thought formed over a period of twenty years were not to be legislated away merely by a formal declaration of separation. Writing became for him at this time primarily, therefore, a means of personal therapy, a medium, as it were, of exorcism through confrontation. We shall see how the need to destroy the apocryphal vision of life which the church had taught him, how the necessity to rid himself of that sense of personal corruption that had been impressed upon him in his early years, was to lead, in *Go Tell*, to a compassionate but nonetheless heretical presentation of the religious life in this novel.

If it is objected that there was something quaintly meretricious in Baldwin's quarrel with God (since such a quarrel could only with great difficulty be made the essential theme of a successful novel) the matter was for him of real and crucial importance. He could not live the life that he so passionately desired, he could not claim for himself that freedom of imagination that was so essential if he was to become a serious artist, so long as his vision of life was so inextricably bound to his medieval sense of dread and sin. But if God was far away in his heaven, if his rebellion against Him was so tragically impractical, there was the memory of his own stepfather—that most formidable of Old Testament patriarchs—against which the would-be writer could vent all his fury, all his rebellion. And it is for this reason that Gabriel Grimes becomes, in *Go Tell*, not simply a reluctant stepfather whose ironically questionable claim to redemption turns him into an egocentric villain, but, more significantly, a personification of the vengeful God of Baldwin's fundamentalist Christian imagination. John Grimes both hates and fears God, but he fears and hates his father with even greater intensity.

But within this pathological relationship there is a touching but un-availing need on his part for love and recognition, from his step-father who for him is not just God's self-proclaimed spokesman on earth but a veritable incarnation of God himself. John's quarrel with God is, then, rendered dramatically plausible through his quarrel with his stepfather, and the creative justification for this painful relationship is provided through the suggestion that the failure of Love is at the root of John's alienation. But if the desperate need for love is a function of John's theophobic predicament in this novel, we must be careful to recognise that there is nothing dogmatic or unduly constricting about the definition of love in this first novel. Homosexuality was in Baldwin's latter novels to be presented often as the exclusively valid category of love, but here its meaning is as much more ramified as it derives ultimately from the Pauline notion of Christian feeling. We shall see later how there is an exquisitely ironic link between the vexatious discomfiture over sexuality in Christian theology and Baldwin's attempt in *Another Country* to celebrate homosexuality as the highest form of love; but we may here distinguish four major categories of love in this first novel. There is the 'erotic' definition (Elizabeth and Richard) that is presented with some degree of sympathy but as having also the least chance of success. (It is conceivable that Baldwin's dark puritan imagination felt rather uneasy about so carnal a love.) There is also the homosexual definition (John and Elisha), the familial definition (Gabriel and John; Gabriel and Elizabeth; Gabriel and Florence), and finally, what may be termed social love—much closer to 'agape' but dealing specifically with the failure of human relationships in society.

If the various categories of love we have here identified are plausible, it becomes clear that *Go Tell* possesses a degree of structural unity that is a fitting testimony to the lessons Baldwin learned during his prolonged apprenticeship. The apparent simplicity of mood that is sometimes seen as the source of this novel's success is, clearly, quite misleading, for its achievement derives not so much from the simplicity of voice or theme, as from the powerful control which Baldwin here exercised over a broad range of thematic concerns. *Go Tell* may be seen as a very subtle essay on the effects of social oppression on a minority group, as an attack on the excesses and snares of black inspirational worship, or as a passionate plea for love in personal relationships. In addition to these perspectives of meaning, the novel can even more significantly be seen as an eloquent record of Baldwin's struggle to break away from his ties to his stepfather's God, from the bondage of theological terror, and the essential achievement of this novel is ultimately not that there are so many perspectives from which it may be seen to have meaning, but that these perspectives coalesce into an astutely integrated vision in which the fear of God and the despair of love are the fundamental forces. John Grimes is afraid of God because he has been persuaded of his own personal corruption (and the God of this novel is a vengeful one)—an equivalent, incidentally, of the black view of whiteness implicit in this novel. But God is ultimately an abstraction against which rebellion can at best be fanciful, and so his stepfather, who in many significant respects *is* God, becomes the actual and visible object of John's fear and hatred. He, however, is not an Iago, and he fears and hates precisely because he so desperately wishes to be loved and recognised. His fear and hatred consequently become intense in proportion to his conviction that love is a real, conceivable possibility, one that he discovers to his chagrin appears to be negated by the ironic power of theological fate. And finally, the negation of the possibility of love on the personal plane, when extended to its communal level, becomes the source both of the pathetic despair of the 'saints' and of racial oppression in American society. Let us examine in some detail the manner in which fear and despair serve as the basic symptoms of Baldwin's rebellion in *Go Tell It on the Mountain*.

Just as love is construed in this novel from varying perspectives, so also does the definition of sin continuously change. Of all the major characters who pray in the Temple, there is not one of them who is not, in some way, guilty of sin, though of course, the enormity of their sins varies from venial to cardinal. If Florence's sin is that of egocentric unbelief and hateful malice against Gabriel, Gabriel's is both carnal and spiritual, for, despite his pretentions to moral rectitude, he is basically incapable of loving anyone. Where Sister McAndless and Praying Mother Washington are presumably guilty of the relatively venial sin of taking themselves too seriously and denying the fulness of life, Elisha's sanctity is apparently contaminated by his innocuous affair with Ella Mae and his apparently sexually motivated love for John. The guilt of sin, however, is not limited merely to the Saints. Indeed, they at least are aware of the promise of redemption, while the rest of 'the world', as represented by the 'sinners along the avenue', is doomed to suffer God's vengeance on the day of reckoning. Part of the dark and critical irony in this situation derives, of course, from the consideration that whereas all the other characters in the novel are guilty of sins of commission, sins that are at any rate subsequent to their existential recognition of the distinction between virtue and vice and over which they therefore have some measure of control, John's sin indeed precedes his birth. It is as though the very circumstances of his conception, let alone his birth, are sufficiently sinful to forever damn him, and there is nothing he can do about his fate. It does not appear to matter that his birth is the one labour of mutual love in the novel, nor that he is the one character for whom love is an absolute necessity. From his first day, it appears, the enormity of this 'sin' is forcefully impressed upon him, and it is hardly surprising that he should grow up both convinced of, and angry over, his fated damnation. Waking up on the morning of his fourteenth birthday, his sense of guilt climaxes in an oppressive feeling of doom. The wages of sin is death, and John convinces himself that nothing can save him:

> This morning not even the cry of a bed-spring disturbed the silence, and John seemed, therefore, to be listening to his own unspeaking doom. He could believe, almost, that he had awakened late on that great getting-up morning; that all the saved had been transformed in the twinkling of an eye, and had risen to meet Jesus in the clouds, and that he was left, with his sinful body, to be bound in hell a thousand years.[2]

The immediate cause of this desperate fear of damnation is, it is true, a harmless enough act of masturbation in the school lavatory, but it is in the nature of Baldwin's concerns here for us to suppose that John's guilt is not merely a putative guilt of the flesh but a more fundamental one that has to do with his desire to disturb the proper relationship between God and man. His sin is not only that he has become aware of his flesh, nor even that he had been born out of wedlock, but that, in refusing to admit his guilt by falling at the feet of God, he had put himself in opposition to God:

> The darkness of his sin was in the hardheartedness with which he resisted God's power; in the scorn that was often his while he listened to the crying, breaking voices, and watched the black skin glisten while they lifted up their arms and fell on their faces before the Lord. For he had made his decision. He would not be like his father, or his father's fathers. He would have another life.[3]

Despite this rebellion, this determination to have another life, John Grimes remains nevertheless as much a victim of his fear of God as those who more willingly concede His power. He cannot, for all his scepticism, entirely rid himself of the suspicion that the penalty for his rebellion is the burning in hell for a thousand years, and because he cannot deny this, he hates even more intensely the vengeful God who so capriciously seeks to confine him to hell.

There is, then, the element of ineluctable fate in John's relationship to his father's God. The one weapon he could employ against this malice was his rebellious imagination, yet this very weapon serves finally only to compound his sense of sin, and in the end God, however unjustly, remains the victor. And so his pathological dread was always to remain more powerfully real than his dreams of escape, even in those brief moments, as in the movie house scene, when he was vividly aware of other possibilities. If his bondage to God is one primarily characterised thus by fear, so also is fear the basic element in his complex relationship to his stepfather Gabriel. Just as John is convinced that God hates him, so also are we given a graphic account of Gabriel's hatred. For the latter, John, with his far from immaculate conception, his bulging devil's eyes, his taciturnity and his rebellious imagination, is the incarnation of the devil. Further, John is not really his son; he is the son of a bondswoman who now threatens to become his heir, since his own true son, Roy, appears to have chosen for himself the path of perdition. Elsewhere in the novel Baldwin does draw the character of Gabriel with appreciably greater compassion, but in the scene in which he describes Gabriel's reaction to Roy's wound, there is no mistaking the searing hatred with which he reenacts his painful life with his own stepfather. Roy is lying on the sofa, having been injured in a street fight. Gabriel returns home from his job and finds him bleeding; and out of his concern for this wayward son he vents his rage on his wife and John:

> More than his words, his face caused John to stiffen instantly with malice and fear. His father's face was terrible in anger, but now there was more than anger in it. John saw now what he had never seen before. . . . a kind of wild, weeping terror that made the face seem younger, and yet at the same time unutterably older and more cruel. And John knew, in the moment his father's eyes swept over him, that he hated John because John was not lying on the sofa where Roy lay.[4]

The point to be made here is that in John's mind there is hardly any distinction between the capriciousness of God's threat to his existence and the intensity of his father's hatred for him. If God had preordained him to burn in hell even before he was born, his father's hatred appears equally to have little to do with whatever sin he may be deemed to have committed; and just as the only defence he has against God is his rebellious imagination, his refusal to concede the power of hell without struggle, so also his only defence against his father is his 'intelligence', the freedom he arrogates to himself to dream at will of the most harrowing revenge:

> That moment gave him, from that time on, if not a weapon at least a shield; he apprehended totally, without belief or understanding, that he had in himself a power that other people lacked, that he could use this to save himself; and that, perhaps, with this power he might one day win that love which he so longed for . . . His father's arm, rising and falling, might make

him cry, and that voice might cause him to tremble; yet his father could never entirely be the victor, for John cherished something that his father could not reach. It was his hatred and intelligence that he cherished.[5]

It is truly remarkable the way in which Baldwin appears in these passages to recognise hardly any distinction between his heavenly and terrestrial fathers. Gabriel, whose very name has obvious significance, is not only John's father but also 'God's minister, the ambassador of the King of Heaven'. To fear and hate him is therefore tantamount to challenging God, as John himself clearly sees: "and John could not bow before the throne of grace without first kneeling to his father"; and precisely because the collusion between these two terrible deities is one against which imaginative rebellion is but specious and ineffective, he is forever doomed to pay the price for his 'sin', a sin doubly compounded by his very attempt to break away from its thrall:

> On his refusal to do this had his life depended, and John's secret heart had flourished in its wickedness until the day his sin overtook him.[6]

Part of the chilling effect that this novel has on the reader derives from the fact that in John's mind, as in Baldwin's, the objects of his fear are ultimately indivisible. In terms of their threat to his existence, there is no significant difference between God, Gabriel, and as we shall see later, the racist society that threatens to destroy him. And in terms of the limited responses available to Baldwin's fictional surrogate in this novel, it is hardly surprising that John's imaginative rebellion against God and Gabriel belongs in the same category as Baldwin's own choice of creative writing as his weapon against the pain of life. Just as God and Gabriel appear to insist on John's corruption, so also does a racist society insist more on his bestiality than on his humanity (and here, we see the manner in which Baldwin manages to draw attention to the theological foundations of racism without at the same time converting this insight into an article of dogma). And if his refusal to kneel before the throne of grace is in the end a specious defence, it is also clear that creative freedom can hardly be seen as the most effective weapon against social injustice. John's dilemma is, then, a vicious one, and the intensity of his hatred is in precise proportion to the enormity of his apparently ineluctable predicament.

Yet there is nothing unduly dogmatic or willful in Baldwin's presentation of imaginative rebellion as a defence against his existential insecurity. Objectively regarded, the response here presented had glaring enough limitations. It is conceivable of course that the writer may move men to act justly and fairly with one another through his fictions, though it would be a vexatious, and perhaps not particularly useful task to seek to determine the relationship between moral counsels and the more formal aspects of a work of art. More pertinent to our discussion here is the consideration that John's response in this novel is a provisional one, in the sense that it is directed less toward resolving his social, than his religious dilemma. As a weapon against an unjust society, the ability to dream of revenge may be an elegant enough symptom of a healthy imagination, but it obviously has very little significance in terms of the practical life that one has to lead. Baldwin was himself later to recognise this, in *Tell Me How Long the Train's Been Gone*, for instance, a novel in which the image of the artist as ultimate rebel yields preeminence to that of the political activist. By the same token also, hatred is a merely negative response, a state of mind that is by no means the necessary and sufficient condition for effective confrontation with social injustice. Baldwin was, again, later to recognise this, in *No Name in the Street*, in which essay he bluntly declares that one does not have to hate one's enemies in order to see the necessity for destroying them. In the context of this novel, in any case, Baldwin does make it clear that one hates precisely because one cannot love or be loved. And in this regard it may be said that a fundamental theme in *Go Tell* is the absurd irrationality of John's undeserved predicament, given, especially, the real possibilities there are for love. The failure of love may then be seen as being at the root of John's despair. The God of this novel is vengeful because he does not truly love; Gabriel is driven by insane and self-consuming hatred because he is incapable of love, and by the same token, the root cause of racism is the failure of love in society. But Baldwin does not merely present these ideas in a dogmatic, rhetorical or polemical manner but rather succeeds in conveying them through the lives and interrelations of his characters. Let us examine, then, the many faces of love, its possibilities and its failures in *Go Tell*.

In the context of Baldwin's despair, the failure of love in this novel in respect of human relationships has its complement in the failure of love with respect to man's relationship to God. The God of this novel is not a long-suffering one. His essential attribute is neither infinite concern nor forbearance. Rather, He is a vengeful and jealous deity whose kingdom is the realm of fear. The saints, when they pray, do so not out of their love for Him but out of fear that he might otherwise hurl his thunderbolts at them. He is not the compassionate God of the New Testament; He does not love. He holds before his worshippers the threat of damnation and the burning in hell for a thousand years, and as has been suggested, Gabriel is not merely God's ambassador on earth; he is indeed God's very incarnation. One does not love Gabriel. One either hates or fears him in proportion to the power he has of punishment over one. Perhaps the only character in the novel who dares to love Gabriel is his mother, who prays to live only for as long as it takes him to realise his potential as a man of God; and it is perfectly ironic that the very realisation of this potential results in Gabriel's denial of his humanity, of his need and capacity for love. Prior to his sanctification, his relationships are distinguished by selfish exploitation. His mother's life appears to have meaning for him only in so far as she serves as a mediator between him and God's anger. Florence herself, while they are living in the South, is the one who takes on both hers and Gabriel's familiar responsibilities. But his essential inhumanity becomes more apparent only, ironically, after his conversion. At this point his family and friends exist for him only as a foil to his sanctimoniousness. He hates his sister, Florence, because she refuses to admit that he is any more virtuous than she is.[7] When he sees her kneeling in tortured prayer in the Temple, he is gratified not because she has at last opened up her heart to God, but because God's vengeance has finally caught up with her and brought her low:

> Gabriel turned to stare at her, in astonished triumph that his sister should at last be humbled . . . She knew that Gabriel rejoiced, not that her humility might lead her to grace, but only that some private anguish had brought her low.[8]

And because Florence knows that the saints are happy over her sudden appearance in the Temple not from love or christian solicitude but from the desire to see her suffer, her prayer is ultimately meaningless, for she dares to believe that those who now stand in gloating judgment over her are no more sinless than she is. Is not Gabriel himself guilty of murder? Had he not stood by in his saintliness while the son of his adulterous passion lived and died in sin? And did he not now hate Elizabeth and John precisely for that sin of which he himself stood guilty? Gabriel is, then, both incapable of love and of charity. He cannot love, nor can he forgive those who dare to love. But it is not that love is impossible of realisation in the world of this novel, though it is difficult enough to achieve and perpetuate. Rather, in the case of Gabriel, the failure of love is a failure in the case of a specific individual, and not one that is attributable to the objective impossibility of it.

But if Gabriel's essential selfishness is an individual limitation rather than the result of an objective dilemma, the relationship between Elizabeth and Richard suggests that there is perhaps a certain arbitrariness in the manner in which Baldwin disposes of the relationships that fall within his various categories of love. If Gabriel does not love because he does not wish to, Richard and Elizabeth fail to perpetuate their love in spite of their desire to do so. Apart from John's love for Elisha, Elizabeth's brief affair with Richard is the one relationship that is presented with less irony than tenderness. They are selfless and considerate, each accepting the other as a human being in his own right. They dream of marital happiness, but Richard dies by his own hand all too soon because society would not have him live. On the one hand, then, it may be argued that Baldwin here intended to dramatize the objective dilemma of being black in America, a dramatization that appears to us so much more plausible because it is illustrated in so private a relationship as the love affair between two young people. On the other hand, however, it is quite possible that Baldwin is here concerned not so much with the racial dimensions of black tragedy as he is preoccupied with his puritan discomfiture over sexual love. It is true that Gabriel can hardly be supposed to be a spokesman for Baldwin in this novel, and it would perhaps be more meaningful to see Gabriel's malice as an indication of the author's intention to present him in as unsympathetic a light as possible; but we shall suggest why this could be a misreading of the situation. Gabriel despises Elizabeth, as he did Deborah, his first wife, because she is in his eyes a 'fallen' woman, and in a certain sense Baldwin is himself as much an inheritor of his father's prejudices as he is a rebel against them. In any case, when we consider the love affair between John and Elisha—and that is what it clearly is, in spite of all the cautiousness of description—it becomes apparent that the argument from social determinism, from racism, is inadequate as an explanation for Richard's untimely death. Elisha and John love each other as much, if more discreetly, as Richard and Elizabeth do, and they are both black and young. Yet their love does not terminate as abruptly as Richard's love for Elizabeth. Indeed, there is the suggestion at the end of the story that their love grows rather than dies. More significantly, if in Gabriel's dreadful theology premarital sex is a sin (and there is no question about this—Elisha is himself admonished for his little harmless affair with Ella Mae), then homosexual love should be even more abominable, since it does not have even the extenuating potential of procreation, and particularly as it seeks to play itself out in the Temple of God. (It is true that Gabriel does not know of the wrestling incident in the Temple, but it is perhaps part of his own obtuseness that he fails to see the erotic element in Elisha's evangelical zeal.) One would expect the God of this novel then to avenge himself on Elisha and John as he presumably did on Richard and Elizabeth. But then, there is the little matter of actual intercourse, and of the innate bestiality of woman. The history of sexual attitudes in Christian thought is a most confusing one indeed, and there is little that is unambiguous to be gained by referring to it for illustration. Nevertheless it is worth observing that Gabriel's (and Baldwin's) attitude to women is little different, for instance, from that of Saint John Chrysostom, who thought that "among all savage beasts none is found so harmful as woman". He was doubtless a neurotic fellow, but his views on sexuality and on women happen to have been quite popular in early Christian thought, and were later to be given a certain legitimacy by Acquinas. Referring to women, he declared that

> . . . the groundwork of this corporeal beauty is nothing else but phlegm and blood and humour and bile . . . when you see a rag with any of these things on it, such as phlegm or spittle, you cannot endure looking at it; are you then in a flutter of excitement about the storehouses and repositories of these things? [9]

There is little need belabouring the point here. Gabriel's disgust with women—with Deborah, with Florence, with the mother of his illegitimate son, and with Elizabeth—does have quite respectable antecedents in christian thought, and in this specific respect his attitude appears to coincide with Baldwin's. Elisha and John survive, and Richard's love for Elizabeth terminates, because despite the 'heresy' implicit in homosexuality, the female involvement in heterosexuality makes it equally, if not more, nauseating. It is not without reason therefore that heterosexual copulation in this novel, as in Baldwin's other novels, is described often as a brutal, indecent spectacle. When Deborah is raped, or when Gabriel makes love to her later; when he sleeps with Esther or the woman from the North, and when John observes his parents in bed, it is always as though we are watching an ugly, distasteful show. The beauty of John's love for Elisha lies, then, apparently in the absence of copulation, and it is possible that Baldwin's puritan imagination saw in this minor distinction a useful alibi for what ultimately appears to be a mere prejudice. The distinction is so obviously absurd that we can only conclude that the author was here denoting a personal preference rather than making an objective comment on the merits of homosexuality.

In view of this confusion with respect to sexuality (a confusion in which Baldwin is clearly not alone) it is more meaningful to see these different dimensions of love—John's love for Elisha, Richard's abortive love for Elizabeth, and Gabriel's rejection of love—primarily as indications of Baldwin's recognition of the possibilities of love. And it is in this sense that *Go Tell It on the Mountain* may be said to be a powerfully idealistic novel, one in which the writer's despair is seen to derive not from the impossibility of an ideal and perfectly blissful relationship between God and man, and among men, but from the corruption of this ideal.[10] In the love between Richard and Elizabeth, between John and Elisha, we are offered glimpses of the ideal relationship, and if, in the end, these intimations do not appear to us to be presented with as much force as the frustrated lives of Florence and Gabriel are, it is less because of a lack of faith on Baldwin's part than because our ideals have a way of often being corrupted by the humdrum reality of our every day lives. Equally, in terms of the broader social perspective of the novel, racism may also be seen as another illustration of the failure of love. If love is in part the willingness to accept the validity of another's life, so is racism the denial of another's humanity. If love implies the ability to forgive, to be charitable, in the christian sense of the term, racial bigotry is equally the inability to show charity and compassion. And it is therefore not surprising that for John Grimes there is ultimately no meaningful distinction between theological and social malice. The God who threatens to consign him to hell is no different from the father who hates him and the society that refuses to concede his right to live. We have seen how, although terrified by his father and by God, yet unwilling to yield without struggle to them, his most potent yet ineffectual weapon against them has been his rebellious imagination. In like manner also, his only defence against the society that seeks to destroy him is his imagination. Just as he dreams of the day when, like the lady in the movie, he would be able to laugh God and his father in the face, so also, on the hill on Central Park in New York, he dreams of the day when he would have the power to humiliate and destroy white America:

He did not know why, but there arose in him an exultation and a sense of power, and he ran up the hill like an engine, or a madman, willing to throw himself headlong into the city that glowed before him . . . Then, he, John, felt like a giant who might crumble this city with his anger; he felt like a tyrant who might crush this city beneath his heel. . . .

Not surprisingly, the power that he longs to possess is not unlike the tyrannous power of God, but it is only a dream, and the reality is both more immediate and more terrifying. Everywhere he went, whatever he did, he could not but be aware of the dangers that awaited him. For white people around him, he did not even have a name. He was a mere excrescence upon the earth, to be despised and humiliated. His father's permanent rage was also in part attributable to the humiliations he suffered at the hands of white America, and God himself appeared to be on the side of those who oppressed and exploited him. If we suspect that there is something overly simplified in John's view of oppression, we must bear in mind that his is a boy's imagination, and that in any case the vision is itself hyperbolic only in detail. The generalization was only too painfully real:

He, John, was a nigger, and he would find out, as soon as he got a little older, how evil white people could be. John had read about the things white people did to colored people; how, in the South, where his parents came from, white people cheated them of their wages, and burned them, and shot them—and did worse things, said his father, which the tongue could not endure to utter. He had read about colored men being burned in the electric chair for things they had not done; how in riots they were beaten with clubs; how they were tortured in prisons; how they were the last to be hired and the first to be fired. Niggers did not live on these streets which John now walked; it was forbidden . . . In John's mind then, the people and the avenue underwent a change, and he feared them and knew that one day he could hate them. . . .[12]

64

It is not that the potential for love in society is inconceivable, as witness the anonymous white man who smiles at John in the park, and the teacher who pays him a reluctant tribute at school, but here again, Baldwin laments not the absence of a conceptual ideal, but the actual corruption of this ideal.

We see then how the possibilities of love, and their corruption, both in the theological and secular sense, may be seen as the organizing principles in this novel. In a very basic sense, *Go Tell* is a painfully sad novel, a novel in which Baldwin testifies to the limitations imposed upon his vision of the infinite possibilities of life by that vengeful triad of loveless forces consisting of God, his father and white society. We may also see the novel as a tenderly lyric celebration of the struggles of such puny mortals as Richard and Elizabeth, John and Elisha, to realise through love their true potential in life. Even Gabriel, who for the most part is presented with an ambiguous feeling of resentment and pity, is occasionally shown as striving in his own fumbling way to love and be loved. Colin McInnes probably overstates the case when he implies that there is more love than sheer egocentric narcissism in Gabriel's relationship to Roy, but he does draw attention to the crux of the matter when he remarks that

. . . deeply as the dramatic and religious elements of the book impress me, I find even more wonderful (Baldwin's) gift for persuading me beyond possibility of doubt that Elizabeth adored Richard, Elisha does love John—and even that poor Gabriel yearns for dead Royal and living Roy.[13]

It is part of the tragedy of this novel that love should be so unconsummated or aborted, yet it is also a mark of Baldwin's provisional triumph over theological and social circumstance that he should thus have even conceived of the possibility of love, given the nature of his experience at the time this novel was written. But it is precisely out of this juxtaposition of hope and despair that true tragedy is made, for to hope in the midst of such formidable sanctions is indeed to testify to one's faith in man's ability to rise above them. Yet this hope, this faith is, if we may believe Baldwin here, in itself an act of rebellion, since it seeks to invalidate the power which external forces, especially theological, have over man. And where the individual who dares thus to dream is one whose mind is consumed, as John's is, by fear of God's vengeance, the rebellion is likely to express itself in primarily theological terms. In this sense then, God, that implacable deity who appears to equate the acceptance of life with sin, is the villain of the piece, with Gabriel, his terrestrial spokesman, and white society—the children apparently created in his image—coming in for secondary condemnation. If God is the villain of this novel, then to dare to love is to rebel against him, and this presumably, is what makes Gabriel such a perfect candidate for God's Kingdom—the fact that he is incapable of loving anyone.

It is not surprising that for Baldwin, in this novel, homosexual love—especially when it seeks to express itself in the Temple of God—is the highest form of rebellious heresy he can conceive of. The body, the Bible tells us, is a temple consecrated to God, and since homosexuality is in this novel expressed for the most part in terms of physical attraction, John apparently sins by trying to substitute Elisha for God. On the occasion of their first meeting in the Temple, it is as though John consciously, if uneasily, exchanges his fear of God for his admiration and love of Elisha:

> But he was distracted by his new teacher, Elisha . . . John stared at Elisha all through the lesson, admiring the timbre of Elisha's voice, much deeper and manlier than his own, admiring the leanness, and grace, and strength, and darkness of Elisha in his sunday suit . . . But he did not follow the lesson, and when, sometimes, Elisha paused to ask John a question, John was ashamed and confused, feeling the palms of his hands become wet and his heart pound like a hammer. Elisha would smile and reprimand him gently, and the lesson would go on.[14]

When, much later, John is lying in psychic pain on the 'threshing floor', it is Elisha's intervention that rescues him from the abyss, and there is an exquisite irony at the end of the story, in the manner in which Elisha's certainty that John has been saved unto God is indeed the very indication of John's conditional release from the power of God's vengeance. Elisha's parting kiss is, to be sure, a holy one, but holy more in the sense that it consecrates a new life, a new beginning, a new religion than that it attests to John's arrival at the throne of grace.[15] The novel ends, then, with Baldwin giving notice of his provisional liberation, of his discovery of a new, more congenial religion, the religion of love. Homosexuality will, for a long time after *Go Tell*, be the medium through which he conveys his alienation from God and society—an alienation, we shall later see, of questionable significance. But apart from the structural achievement of this novel, Baldwin's more limited triumph here is the manner in which, by objectifying the details of his past, he succeeds in making apparent his preliminary liberation from theological terror. That this liberation brought with it another kind of insecurity, another challenge, both in terms of his uneasiness over the value of employing homosexuality either as symbolic or actual rebellion, and in terms also, of the necessity he must have recognised to deal more specifically with his social dilemma, we shall see in the following chapters; but it is useful here to observe that though there is in this novel a measure of social criticism implicit in Baldwin's critique of his past, political issues and concerns were secondary to his primarily theological preoccupation here, and it was to take him three novels, two plays and a large number of essays to come to grips with the more public aspects of his dilemma in the Western world.

Notes to Chapter Three

1. Lionel Trilling, 'The Fate of Pleasure', in *Beyond Culture,* Viking Press, 1963, p. 56 ff.
2. Baldwin, *Go Tell It on the Mountain,* Dell, 1955, p. 18
3. ibid., p. 19
4. ibid., pp. 42–43
5. ibid., pp. 20–21

6. ibid.
7. ibid., p. 89
8. ibid., p. 65
9. cited in Arno Karlen, *Sexuality and Homosexuality: A New View*, W. W. Norton, 1971, p. 70
10. *Go Tell* may also be seen as an 'anti-utopian' novel, as a novel that deals with the vulgarization of christian theology and the corruption of the ideal human relationship. Baldwin appears to assume that in an ideal state man need not fear God nor hate his fellow man, but that we have failed, with tragic consequences to ourselves, to achieve our potential. For our definition of the anti-utopian novel, see Irving Howe, 'The Fiction of Anti-Utopia,' in Sheldon Grebstein, op. cit., p. 220 ff.
11. Baldwin, *Go Tell*, p. 33.
12. ibid., pp. 36–37
13. Colin McInnes, 'Dark Angel: The Writings of James Baldwin,' *Encounter*, vol. 21 (Aug. 1963), No. 2, pp. 22–23
14. Baldwin, *Go Tell*, p. 13
15. ibid., pp. 220–21

Four

The Pain Examined

76-82

D. H. Lawrence once remarked that a fundamental limitation of modern tragedy was that in it man was no longer at war with God, his sense of conflict being limited only to his alienation from society,[1] and though the context of this remark suggested a rather typical Lawrentian caprice, the observation was itself one that few critics could take exception to. In American literature, at any rate, time was when to offer even a fictional critique of man and his life implied, almost inevitably, a certain stance with respect to God. One could speak in serious critical terms of Melville's quarrel with God, of Hawthorne's theological ambiguities, and, more recently, of Hemingway's increasingly daring attempts to substitute another canon of morality for that way of life that was allegedly founded on christian principles of varying degrees of usefulness. The latter popularization of Freudian determinism, and of that mode of political and social thought deriving mainly from Hegel's post-religious philosophy has led to that category of imaginative critiques of man-in-society in which the decline of the sacred, of the divine order, is taken as the point of departure rather than as the legitimate context of the creative vision. But if it is true that we have in the twentieth century witnessed the decline of the religious imagination (which is not quite the same thing as the decline of religious terminology or symbolism) Baldwin is without doubt an exception to this generalization, as are indeed, not a few black writers in this country. It would certainly be rewarding to enquire into the reasons for the paradoxical survival of the religious imagination in black culture and literature, paradoxical both in the sense that it is the single most significant explanation for black survival in this country, and because it is the one mode of consciousness that most politically vocal groups in the black community today are agreed is an uncomfortable liability that obstructs their attempts to clarify the political issues in society. More specifically, we have seen how, in *Go Tell It on the Mountain*, John Grimes' fear and hatred of God is ultimately indistinguishable from his fear and hatred of society, and by the same token, it would be impossible to make any meaningful observations on Baldwin's second novel, *Giovanni's Room*, without taking account of its theological perspective. It is true that in his own remarks on this novel, Baldwin had given the impression that he was primarily concerned with the psychosexual perspectives of David's dilemma. "David's dilemma," he had argued, "is the dilemma of many men of his generation, by which I do not so much mean sexual ambivalence as a crucial lack of sexual authority." [2] Were one obliged to accept the post factum observations of writers on their works as received truth, it would have to be admitted that there is an obvious level of psycho-social meaning in this novel, a level in which we may understand Baldwin to imply in the remark above a broadly sociological interpretation of sexual abnormality and its consequences. And in this regard it would then be necessary to point to the evidence of David's childhood, to the fact that his father is an inadequately authoritative figure, that in his dreams he is obsessed by a repulsive yet vaguely erotic vision of his dead mother. On the strength of this evidence, one may conceivably conclude that David is merely a victim of certain determinisms, social and historical. But the limitations of so vulgarly Freudian an explanation become quite apparent once we consider the case of Giovanni. There is even less evidence in the novel to suggest any seriously psychosocial explanation for Giovanni's ambivalence. The culture into which he was born is presumably a healthily virile one, one in which such sexual deviations in men are frowned upon. Secondly, though the fact itself does not preclude sexual ambivalence, Giovanni was once happily married, and the reasons for his departure from his family had nothing to do with his sexual behaviour. Indeed, the economic perspective of Giovanni's homosexuality is perhaps even more significant than the psychological, but it seems more reasonable to suggest that it is in Baldwin's religious imagination that we shall find the source of his preoccupations in this novel. And if this is the case, it may well be that this is not so much a novel *about* homosexuality as it is one that deals with the implications of homosexuality in a cosmology that is buttressed on a terrified vision of the relationship between man and God.

On the other hand, *Giovanni's Room* is obviously in some sense a novel about 'love,' and though there is often a strong temptation to see this novel as an odd piece in the Baldwin canon, it is instructive to consider also that in terms of their thematic scope, and despite the all-too-insistent absence of black characters in the latter novel, *Go Tell* and *Giovanni's Room* belong inseparably together. If the failure of love is seen as a major theme in the first novel, we have earlier suggested that this failure is so demonstrated as to leave us with the impression that its possibility still exists in spite of the painful and more dramatic reality of its corruption or negation. There is an open-endedness about the conclusion of this first novel which suggests that Baldwin had hardly exhausted his examination of the theme of love, and he himself was later to observe that in writing *Giovanni's Room* he had felt impelled to reopen his examination of this crucial conundrum.[3] In any case, when John Grimes walks up the steps of his parents' home believing that he has at last been 'saved,' we are persuaded that his salvation is less unto God than into a new, substitute religion, the religion of love. Yet in spite of, or perhaps because of, John's tender euphoria it is clear that he has as yet not fully examined the implications of his salvation, the guilt that arises from a sense of one's rebellion against God, the enormous expenditure of emotional and spiritual vigor necessary to sustain the new religion, the painful duality that comes from that apparently inevitable quest for freedom which in turn leads to the corruption of innocence, and finally, the irrevocable sense of existential rootlessness that results from the attempt to substitute a religious certainty, however irksome, with a more secular yet equally problematic faith. When David walks away from the mirror at the end of the story in *Giovanni's Room*, he may very well have discovered the sanctity of his naked flesh—a discovery that in the context of this novel is a daring and crucial one—but his apprehension of the disaster that he believes is the sequel to this revelation appears to us a more forceful reality than his discovery. His final statement, we shall see later, is less a lyrical declaration of hope and faith than it is a desperate prayer for that grace which he formerly rejected, and it is because of this unresolved juxtaposition of hope (which in this context is synonymous with rebellion) and despair that the issue is at least once again to be reopened in *Another Country*, though by this time love has ceased to be merely a principle of private relationships and has become the postulated dynamic of more communal ties.

Baldwin had already begun work on *Another Country* when he decided to complete writing on *Giovanni's Room*, and this decision is in itself quite instructive. The unmediated progression from the primarily apolitical concerns of *Go Tell* to the more 'social' preoccupations of *Another Country* may have proved too burdensome, and it was probably necessary for him to buy time, as it were, by remaining for a while within the limits of his own private dilemma. At any rate, between the appearance of *Go Tell* and of *Another Country*, he produced, apart from a play, two major works: *Giovanni's Room* and his first collection of essays, *Notes of a Native Son*, both of which were significant more for their concern to clarify, if not resolve, the limits of this personal dilemma than for their attempt to deal with the more public issue of Baldwin's political fate as a black man in America. And it is precisely because of this preoccupation with a personal predicament that David, the hero of *Giovanni's Room* is, despite his colour, just as unmistakable a surrogate for Baldwin as John Grimes is—and this must surely be one of the more extreme examples in contemporary literature of a writer's attempt to maintain a certain distance from his subject matter through the objectification of his experience.

Giovanni's Room is not a novel that deals primarily with homosexuality, nor is it, at least in terms of Susan Sontag's definition of the pornographic imagination, a pornographic one.[4] Though Giovanni and Hella and David are in a limited sense interchangeable sexual objects, the novel does not really indulge in that celebration of sexuality in which everything is reducible and meaningful only in so far as it is capable of providing erotic pleasure. It is true that we see the major characters of this novel quite often only in the context of their sexual lives, but far from suggesting that the sexual life has any kind of exclusive validity or that it is an exclusively useful paradigm of the essence of life, it is as though Baldwin were in fact anxious to demonstrate to us the desperation and the squalor that are the logical outcome of his characters' morbidity. Giovanni is ironically the one who pays the extreme penalty, but neither Guillaume nor Jacques, David nor even Hella escapes that profound spiritual despair, the loneliness which Baldwin, perhaps unconsciously, appears to postulate as the inevitable price these characters have to pay for their daring to snatch their sense of freedom from received morality. One of the major preoccupations of this novel is therefore not really an attempt to provide a description of the pornographic sensibility, but more significantly a concern to resolve the problem of personal 'freedom'—and we must be careful to understand the specific usage of this term here. When Baldwin talks of freedom he often refers, not to a political idea but to a mental or spiritual state of being. Freedom, in this novel, is a state of rebellion; to claim it is to assert the individual's ability to reject received morality, an assertion that is tantamount to a rejection of God. When John Grimes in the earlier novel attains the state of 'salvation,' we have suggested that this salvation is a deceptive one, that what he actually attains is, not a reconciliation with his father's God, but a discovery of the at least theoretical possibility of standing *away* from God. But where this heretical stance is in *Go Tell* primarily a tentative one—one that is conceived of only in the mind—the stance in *Giovanni's Room* is a much more empirical one. When David recalls his earlier life with Hella, it is not the *dream* of freedom that he remembers, but its actualization. As he recalls,

I was thinking of our nights in bed, of the peculiar innocence and confidence, which will never come again, which had made those nights so delightful, so unrelated to past, present, or anything to come, so unrelated, finally, to my life since it was not necessary for me to take any but the most mechanical responsibility for them.[5]

73

On the one hand, freedom lay in the ability to act with 'confidence' and without responsibility, but on the other hand, such a condition was possible only in so far as one was willing to act as an absolutely autonomous being, as an entity sufficient unto itself. But such a condition is in practical terms clearly inconceivable, and so freedom becomes more properly the exchange or substitution of 'mooring-posts,' in the context of this novel the substitution of dependence on Hella and Giovanni for subjugation unto God. Furthermore, enslavement to Joey or Hella or Giovanni may be more tolerable than enslavement to God, but finally David comes to feel that the very act of substitution, the attempt to replace God, is in itself of extremely dubious advantage: freedom may be for him an assertion of his vitality, of his uniqueness as a human being, but it appears to bring with it an often unbearable sense of guilt. In a certain sense, of course, David's dilemma is self-created and somewhat fictitious, for in his mind the assertion of man's freedom appears to be synonymous with the commission of sin. He appears incapable of conceiving of the possibility of defining freedom beyond the context of his religious dread, and so he comes to the somewhat rhetorical conclusion that "nothing is more unbearable, once one has it, than freedom", and in a passage so acutely reminiscent of Hemingway, goes on to add that "life (for which read God) gives these and also takes them away and the great difficulty is to say Yes to life." [6]

It is, ironically, an indication of the intensity of Baldwin's struggle at this time to break away from the bonds of theological terror that his sense of guilt and sin appear here to be more real than his anticipation of release. It is significant, for instance, to consider the manner in which David is at once anxious for emancipation and yet so irretrievably bound to his somewhat medieval sense of personal corruption. His boyish, one-night affair with Joey is one that, to minds less entangled in religious fear, would mean little more than a passing recognition of man's latent bisexuality, but for David it is much more than that. It is a corrupt and shameful act that he cannot bear to recall, but which he is at the same time unable to forget. So intense is his conception of sin that this quite forgettable affair is blown up into a major catastrophe. There is no mistaking the prevalence of the imagery of corruption that runs through Baldwin's description of David's state of mind after the affair with Joey:

> The incident with Joey had shaken me profoundly and its effect was to make me secretive and cruel. I could not discuss what had happened to me with anyone, I could not even admit it to myself; and, while I never thought about it, it remained nevertheless, at the bottom of my mind, as still and as awful as a decomposing corpse. And it changed, it thickened, it soured the atmosphere of my mind.[7]

The incident with Joey, then, is the one ineffaceable, cardinal sin, the one single act of alienation, the point of departure from which every subsequent incident in his life appears to him to derive meaning. Having once been infected by this 'sin,' nothing else he does can erase the enormity of this primal crime. And it is in the context of David's passionate need to convince himself that he is not inherently corrupt that we must consider his subsequent affair with Hella.

It is not at all clear from David's account of this relationship that he is ever in love with Hella, nor does she herself ever give the impression or imagine that she is in love with him. In a sense they both exploit each other, and as David himself admits, they appear to be attracted to each other precisely because they are so much in need of 'mooring-posts.' The relationship develops in two stages. The first is the stage of sexual abandonment, the days and nights of unmitigated passion. There is a rather curious dialectic in the content of this relationship. David and Hella get together in Paris partly because sex is fun, but more significantly because, far removed in a foreign land from the eyes of their parents and society, they can afford almost anonymously to assert themselves as 'free' human beings.[8] Yet because of this surfeit of freedom, they are not responsible to each other and so may depart at will. And so the irresponsibility of their relationship drives them, apparently, into the desire voluntarily to limit the scope of their freedom. But this desire is by no means an indication either of mutual concern or of respect.

It is motivated not by the wish to protect, but by a selfish fear of the future. Hella's letter from Spain is certainly not the most romantic of love letters, and once one wades through all its girlish facetiousness, it becomes clear that she is frightened by the infinite possibilities that her notion of freedom implies. "The trouble," she writes from Spain, "is that I love myself too much. And so I have decided to let two try it, this business of loving me, I mean, and see how that works out." [9] There is something altogether too silly and trivial about Hella, and we are not at all persuaded that such a relationship as she wants with David has any chance of success, nor does she herself appear to expect it to succeed. She wants to be married because she does not wish to age into promiscuous senility like the old lascivious hags she meets in Spain, and David wants to marry Hella as material proof of his normality, as convincing evidence that he does not belong to 'le milieu,' the fraternity of bloodless homosexuals of Parisian night life. And it might all have worked, had Hella not gone off to Spain and left David free to meet Giovanni.

Giovanni is the last person in the world with whom a man of David's moral ambiguities could safely afford to have anything to do. Perhaps the most developed character in the novel, and certainly the most sympathetic, his passionate life is the very antithesis of the chill, puritan hypocrisy which David is heir to. It is not that he is blissfully unaware of sin, that he is a noble and innocent savage, nor that his passion is an unreflecting one. Rather, he is David's nemesis, and in a more limited sense his salvation, precisely because he refuses to conceive of any meaningful existence that is devoid of a conception of sin. His arrival in Paris is in itself an act of rebellion against the pious little moralities of his Italian village, and he is certainly not unacquainted with the mythology of Heaven and Hell. In a profound sense, he is the one who has really suffered at the hands of fate, the one who has had to bear, not merely the pain of mental uncertainty, but the pain of life itself. As he himself exclaims in one of his more disturbed moments, his suffering in Paris appears to him to be divine punishment for his own sins:

I left my village and I came to this city where surely God has punished me for all my sins and for spitting on his holy son, and

76

where I will surely die. I do not think that I will ever see my village again.[10]

Giovanni, then, is not 'innocent'; he is not unacquainted with the theology of sin and retribution. Indeed, there is a touching pathos in the literalness of his acceptance of the proposition that the wages of sin is death. In a sense, of course, he is an old stereotype, the credulous and emotional Southern swain, for whom heaven and hell are nothing if not palpable realities. It must, however, be emphasized that, fatalistic though he may be, his fatalism is a much more robust, much more virile one, certainly to our mind, much more sympathetic than David's rather contrived, elegant sense of despair. He is the one who dares David to be alive, the one who challenges him to think of his body as a very vital component of his essence, and not as a "decomposing corpse." It is not that he thinks the flesh is incorruptible, as witness his feeling of revulsion when Guillaume, the cafe owner, touches or looks at him. Rather, he believes that love, even physical love, has the redemptive power of purifying the flesh, that two men can derive from each other an essential joy which Hella could never begin to comprehend, let alone give. And so when he bursts out in rage against David, it is only partly out of desperation, but more significantly out of anger at David's cowardice:

You do not love anyone! You never have loved anyone, I am sure you never will! You love your purity, you love your mirror —you are just like a little virgin . . . You think you came here covered with soap—and you do not want to *stink*, not even for five minutes, in the mean time . . . You want to leave Giovanni because he makes you stink. You want to despise Giovanni because he is not afraid of the stink of love. You want to kill him in the name of all your lying little moralities. And you—you are immoral. You are, by far, the most immoral man I have met in all my life.[11]

It is one of the finer qualities of this novel that Baldwin thus manages to communicate in searing dialogue what in straightforward narrative would have been quite tedious to read. David is everything Giovanni says he is. At once daring and cowardly, rebellious yet terrified of the consequences of his rebellion, he is a man torn and tortured between his desires and the 'lying little moralities' that turn his passion into inertia. He loves Giovanni, as he had loved Joey, but persuades himself that it is a filthy kind of love. It is significant to observe the numerous occasions in the story when his awareness of reality is circumscribed by the imagery of filth and putrefaction. When his father invites him to return home, it reminds him, he reports, of the 'sediment at the bottom of a stagnant pond.' Guillaume's grotesqueness makes him uneasy, 'perhaps in the same way that the sight of monkeys eating their own excrement turns some people's stomach.' [12] Living with Giovanni is filthy and dirty, and carnal love with Sue is even more repulsive. Nothing more dramatically illustrates David's sense of corruption than his view of Giovanni's room. The room is, to be sure, not a particularly livable one, cluttered as it is with dilapidating furniture and discarded boxes. His description of the room's shabbiness is real enough, and though it may be, as Colin McInnes has observed, the symbol of sterility and decay, its presumed metaphysical connotations exist only in David's mind.[13] What is to us more curious is his somewhat precious attempt to project this material filth into an exclusive reflection of the filth in Giovanni's mind. "This was not," he remarks, "the garbage of Paris, which would have been anonymous: this was Giovanni's regurgitated life." [14] Giovanni himself certainly finds his own room extremely unpleasant, but for him it is simply a physical reality, the result of his poverty, a reflection of his economic status, not some arcane symbol of an inner spiritual decay. And so, as we read the intensity of David's revulsion—

Under this blunted arrow, this smashed flower of light lay the terrors which encompassed Giovanni's soul. I understood why Giovanni had wanted me and had brought me to his last retreat. I was to destroy this room and give to Giovanni a new and better life[15]—

as we observe David desperately seeking to pose as Giovanni's redeemer, we begin to suspect that what is happening here is a disingenuous process of projection, that what David seeks to do is transfer, in all his unconvincing self-righteousness, onto Giovanni's life the guilt and desperation in his own soul. Giovanni is, to be sure, a desperate enough man. He is not averse to the tricks of the confidence man. He is, after all, a young European, and deliberately sets out to capture his innocent American cousin. His propensity to violence, even when merely verbalized, is only barely held in check most of the time. He is hard, sometimes coyly amorous, sometimes deliberately brutal. And he does not think too much of women. But we must draw a necessary distinction between his despair and David's. Giovanni's despair is not, like David's, that of the theologically damned; rather, his is the despair of the economically dispossessed. Where David can rely on the occasional check from home, Giovanni has most of the time to live on his wits for lack of meaningful employment. Further, he is certainly not a stranger to theological terror, but rarely does he allow his fear of God's vengeance to destroy his passion for life. Despite his emotionalism, his awareness of the complexity (or the chaos) of life rests more easily on him than it does on David, and it is precisely because of this awareness that his desire to impose some semblance of order on the pattern of his life, if only through homosexual love, is not for him a filthy degenerate quest but a veritable quest for virtue. In a word, Giovanni belongs to the twentieth century; his awareness of the divine order of things, of the sacred, impresses us much less than his rationalistic imagination. His moral predicament derives more directly from the economic and social stratifications of our age than from his thraldom to the theology of fear. It is therefore an indication again—perhaps the most telling one in this story—of Baldwin's theophobic preoccupations at this time that he should here have failed to develop the clearly economic perspective of Giovanni's predicament in this novel.

David, on the other hand, belongs only partially to our century. He is by no means affluent (and here one may congratulate Baldwin for avoiding the temptation of turning David into a typically wealthy, and vulgar, American tourist in Europe) but he does have an advantage over Giovanni—he does not have to work. The fact that he takes this crucial difference for granted is an indication both of his basic egocentricity and of his preoccupation with religious dreads. Innocent of the true meaning of poverty, of the depths of degradation to which hunger can drive even the most well-meaning of men, he can well afford the time for theoretical disquisitions on the nature of virtue and of freedom, and it is this fundamental innocence that makes him guilty of the callousness of which Giovanni charges him. It is this innocence, again, that enervates him, and leads him to refuse to concede that life need be complex, or that man need be the repository of unresolvable ambiguities. His is a form of perhaps involuntary hypocrisy that gives rise both to moral cowardice and to inhumanity. Neither in his affair with Hella nor in his life with Giovanni do we see him demonstrate a sincerely selfless concern for his mate, and to the extent that he learns anything from his sojourn in Paris, it is precisely this lesson that Giovanni forces him to learn, that to love and to be fallibly human need not constitute a sin. Without dwelling (with Robert Bone) on such issues as who is the true priest and who the neophyte in this novel, we may at least observe that it is not at all certain, at the end of the story—and despite Giovanni's tragic suicide—that David achieves that liberation from theological terror which is of the essence of his quest in this novel. When Giovanni is about to die, we see David standing naked before a mirror and reflecting on his life. And as we share his thoughts, we are not persuaded that there has been any real change in him, from the time of his feelings of guilt over the affair with Joey to the more recent incident of Giovanni's collapse. It may or may not be true, as Fern Eckman suggests, paraphrasing Baldwin, that the moral of David's life is that "the man who struggles to preserve his innocence is doomed to sink into corruption." [16] What is of greater importance is that David appears not to have gained much from his experience. In the end he is just as unwilling to live with his ambiguities, just as numbed by his fear of God, as he is at the beginning. He speaks of the longing to be free as though unaware that freedom rests precisely on one's willingness to accept one's experience; he appears to have inherited Giovanni's fatalism without the robust equanimity that made the latter's so much more plausible. "I look at my sex," he reflects, "my troubling sex, and I wonder how it can be redeemed, how I can save it from the knife. The journey to the grave is already begun, the journey to corruption is, always, already, half over." [17] And then he concludes his reflections with an assertion of faith which to us appears not so much an indication of return to the old verities as it is an expression of his bondage to the theology of dread:

I must believe, I must believe that the heavy grace of God, which has brought me to this place, is all that can carry me out of it.[18]

Except, then, in so far as David's life in *Giovanni's Room* is a much more pragmatic attempt to examine the limits and possibilities of his new religion, of his rebellion, the conclusions to be derived from Baldwin's second novel are not, in essence, dissimilar to the implications of John Grimes' life in *Go Tell It on the Mountain*. Rebellion, Baldwin seems to argue, is on the individual plane a most vexatious conundrum. It is just as much the source of inner vitality as it is fraught with countless dangers, for the man who dares to rebel against God has to live perpetually with the threat of damnation. In any case, what is quite clear is that up till the time of the publication of *Giovanni's Room*, Baldwin was still preoccupied with the anatomy of theological terror, but from an intensely personalized perspective. Clearly he must have felt that he needed to resolve, or at least to understand the scope of his private dilemma before he could begin to deal with the more public, social aspects of his alienation. It was, ironically, in the nature of such an adventure that he was doomed to fail to provide any answers, precisely because he could distinguish between his public and private dilemma only theoretically, by an arbitrary act, as it were, of creative will. Indeed, if we find *Go Tell* a more successful novel than *Giovanni's Room* it is partly because there is in the first novel a much more organic integration of Baldwin's theological and secular concerns, whereas *Giovanni's Room* is much more limited in thematic scope, a precious but nonetheless whimsical flirtation with morbidity. The latter novel does, of course, have its moderate successes. It is, after all, one of the few novels in America in which the homosexual sensibility is treated with some measure of creative seriousness, and,

81

furthermore, there is a measure of lyricism in the story that recommends it to the sympathetic reader. Nevertheless it is, and despite the autobiographical elements in it, something of an oddity, a fanciful romantic dalliance that still served the quite important purpose of allowing its author the time he apparently needed to move toward a more public position in his art. Baldwin's theological terror was never to be entirely exorcised, but in his subsequent works he was able more successfully to subsume it within an increasingly primary concern with more public themes. In the next chapter we shall show how, after *Giovanni's Room*, he began to move farther away from a theological definition of man.

Notes to Chapter Four

1. D. H. Lawrence, *The Posthumous Papers*, ed. Edward W. MacDonald, Viking, 1936, p. 420
2. Baldwin, cited in Eckman, op. cit., p. 113
3. ibid.
4. Susan Sontag, 'The Pornographic Imagination,' *Styles of Radical Will*, Farrar, Straus, 1969, esp. pp. 67–68
5. Baldwin, *Giovanni's Room*, Dell, 1956, p. 9
6. ibid., p. 10
7. ibid., p. 24
8. ibid., pp. 9–10
9. ibid., p. 124
10. ibid., p. 185
11. ibid., pp. 186–87
12. ibid., p. 39
13. Colin McInnes, op. cit., pp. 27–28
14. Baldwin, *Giovanni's Room*, p. 114
15. ibid., pp. 115–116
16. Eckman, op. cit., p. 113
17. Baldwin, *Giovanni's Room*, p. 223
18. ibid., pp. 223–24

Five

Baldwin's Blueprint for a New World

In a formal sense, *Go Tell It on the Mountain* was a difficult production for Baldwin. It was his first published novel, one in which he attempted to demonstrate his competence as a novelist, to justify himself, as he was later to observe, to those who wondered if he could really become a writer.[1] The controlled lyricism, the tightly knit form, and the dramatic intensity of this novel were the performance of an already accomplished 'writer,' a writer, that is, who was quite aware of the more formal, aesthetic necessities of art. He had had to go through a painful and often unrewarding apprenticeship of more than a decade to learn this, and it had not made matters any less difficult that the subject he had chosen as the medium of his initiation into Parnassus had been an intensely private one—one too, that exposed him rather helplessly to the snares of sentimentality. To rely as heavily as Baldwin had done in this first novel on one's own personal history, especially when this involved a painful, deprived childhood and an adolescence that was rendered almost unbearable by the facts of racial discrimination and malice, could very easily have led to an unconscious desire on the writer's part to compel the reader merely to pity. But Baldwin did manage to escape this temptation; we do not feel pity for most of the characters in this novel. We are astonished, rather, by the simple, embattled courage of their lives, by the manner in which, through various strategies, they manage to survive, if not triumph over the bitter limitations imposed upon their lives by external forces in society. Baldwin avoided the danger of undue sentimentality in this novel by objectifying his experience to a certain degree, by implying, rather than declaring, the crucial significance of the racial issue for the lives of his characters. But this objectification of his experience laid him open, in turn, to another equally real danger, the danger of his novel becoming the sport of readers and critics intent on what Miss Sontag would call 'interpretation.' It was tempting enough to see John Grimes' private dilemma in this novel as paradigmatic of a more public crisis, a microcosm, as it were, of the crisis of love in the world at large. The implications were there, of course, and real enough, for there is a limited sense in which one can see John's condition not only as symbolic of, but indeed as coterminous with a broader social malaise; but it would clearly have been quite misleading to isolate the social implications of this first novel from its author's major preoccupation here, which was, put simply, to exorcise his dread of hell through an imaginative return to the fields of his psychic wound. In any case, however, one of the more lasting impressions that one is left with on reading this novel is that it is ingeniously inconclusive. It states the hypothesis that love is both tragically lacking in society and also quite possible of attainment, but it does not offer us any dramatically sustained examination of this potentiality. It plots out, rather vaguely, the inner limits of Baldwin's definition of love, and insinuates that to dare to love is a veritable act of rebellion against a certain conception of God; but we leave the novel feeling that John's euphoric sense of salvation is too brief a summing up of a much more complex situation. And if we are to accept Baldwin's own account of the matter, *Go Tell* was, at least in retrospect, a consciously inconclusive novel. "I knew," he later observed, "that I had more to say and much, much more to discover than I had been able to indicate in *Mountain*." [2]

In *Another Country*, his third novel, he was to refer to the need to explore 'the unexamined pain,' but the process of examination begins much earlier, in his second novel, *Giovanni's Room*. It is John Grimes' putative salvation, his discovery of the possibility of freedom from the terror of hell (the hero in this novel, to be sure, is now called David, and he is white and therefore free of the additional pain of racial malice) that is under examination. For if John's provisional triumph lay in his cognitive discovery of freedom, it was David's later burden to discover, through action, that

84

freedom can be a most vexatious acquisition. But though Baldwin attempted in his second novel to provide a more detailed examination of the practical implications of love and freedom, this novel was nevertheless much less of a success mainly because it turned out to be the record of an exquisitely encapsulated vision. The hero of this novel appears to be more concerned with denying his ever present history than with accommodating it. It is not that he is a historiless individual, as Hemingway's embattled heroes tend to be (it is David's past, for instance, that drives him to Paris and into Giovanni's arms) but he appears determined to exorcise his past away by mere fiat, and his final demoralisation arises precisely from this fundamental inability to come to terms with his experience. Furthermore, it is worth observing that *Giovanni's Room* does not fail because the experience recorded in it is false or unreal—and this despite the fact that all the characters in it are white —but rather because the world in which they act out their roles is too rarefied, the canvas of their lives too thin. In a sense, a major inadequacy in the novel comes from Baldwin's failure to lend sufficient weight to the socio-economic perspectives of Giovanni's despair, and because of this failure, this vacuum, his second major fictional effort became a *tour de force,* a commendable architechtonic exercise almost entirely devoid of purposeful seriousness.

Technically, then, *Go Tell* and *Giovanni's Room* were competent novels, the former much more effective than the latter; in them Baldwin had given sufficient demonstration of his ability to control the fictional form, which he had so far employed to communicate the enormity of his private dread. Partly because of his limited objectives in these two novels, and partly also because of his very need to exorcise his theological terror, he began to acquire the reputation of a writer preoccupied with complex but nonetheless rather esoteric psychic conditions.[3] There was the danger that the specifics of the acclaim he was beginning to win, both at home and abroad, were likely to become the very source of his creative stagnation, and he himself was well aware that a writer's greatest tragedy came when he began to imitate himself.[4] If we see his development from an evolutionary standpoint, and given his own awareness of the dangers of self-imitation, it becomes clear that the movement from the internalized realms of *Go Tell* and *Giovanni's Room* to the furious rage of *Another Country*'s more externalized canvas was, then, inevitable. It was the natural development for a writer who had become at least theoretically convinced that art was less isolation than communion, that however intrinsically valid the exploration of a private world may be, it was nevertheless self-limiting constantly to impose on his art a vision of life that did not immediately elicit recognition from his readers. As he later remarked,

> I thought the thing to do, if you're really terribly occupied with
> . . . yourself . . . is to, at any price whatever . . . get in touch
> with something more than you . . . Throw yourself into a situa-
> tion where you won't have time to weep.[5]

Not long after the publication of *Giovanni's Room* Baldwin did have both reason and opportunity to throw himself into situations. The Supreme Court decision of 1954 had helped dramatize the ugly racial animosities in the American psyche which most liberals were unwilling to be reminded of, and in the wake of the critical situation that developed in the South, Baldwin felt obliged to terminate his self-imposed exile in France and return to the United States. It was, he concluded, all well and good to indulge in 'elegant despair,' far removed from the scenes of racial conflict, but a writer for whom moral integrity was of the utmost importance could not justifiably pontificate from a distance on the viciousness of racism while removed and comfortably protected from its immediate effects. He returned to America and threw himself into something of an activist role, frequently visiting and writing about the South and the condition of black people both in the North and South. He was later to record this harrowing experience in *No Name in the Street*, but in terms of the development of his social consciousness his experience of the South at this time was the one catalyst his imagination needed to fuse his private visions with his awareness of more public issues. Almost overnight, he became a spokesman for the dispossessed, his observations more poignantly angry, his public statements more direct and embittered. It is of crucial importance to observe, however, that this very process of radicalization appears to have inversely affected his competence as an artistic craftsman. *Another Country*, the creative testament to his emergence from isolation, was by far a much more significant work than *Giovanni's Room*, but it was at the same time rather less successful as art. There were many reasons for this.

In terms of its conception, *Another Country* was a much more ambitious novel than either *Go Tell* or *Giovanni's Room*. It sought to encompass and to more fully examine the roots of America's social malaise. Love, or the absence of it, which in the earlier novels had for the most part been presented as a matter of individual relationships, became in this novel a much more serious social issue. Its ramifications on the canvas of American life were no longer merely insinuated, but dramatized within the context of interracial relationships. Furthermore, it was not without significance that for the first time Baldwin was in this novel beginning to move away from his vision of man as Homo Theologicus, that his characters were becoming increasingly unaware of the existence of the vengeful God of the earlier novels. This conceptual departure was by no means, however, a clear indication that he had entirely renounced the old cosmology, or that his religious imagination was now in utter abeyance. There is indeed reason to believe that part of the weakness of this novel derives from the probability that his delivery from theological terror was as yet still ambiguous. What the conceptual departure did mean in practical terms was that Baldwin had deliberately taken upon himself a vastly larger scope of material as the subject matter of his creative concerns—a feat he had never before attempted—and in view of the ambiguousness of his liberation from the cosmology of terror, it was not altogether surprising that he should ultimately have failed to provide a sufficiently integrated vision in *Another Country*.

Secondly, *Another Country* was the first of Baldwin's novels in which anger serves a quite specific structural function. Ida Scott is, quite simply, the personification of Baldwin's rage, and as we shall see later, this personified rage in conjunction with Rufus' life and suicide provides Baldwin with a useful instrument for plausibly achieving the self-confrontation of the other characters in the novel. The fiery rage that burns through the pages of this novel was both necessary and inevitable, given the nature of the experience that its author relied upon, but it must also be remarked that the fury of *Another Country* is volatile, elemental, and is often construed as an end in itself, rather than as a structural means by which certain behavioural conflicts are resolved. Despite Baldwin's apparent intention of employing anger as a vehicle of meaning, the two most angry characters in the novel, Rufus and Ida, are in fact the least sympathetic. Ironically, one is confronted with a curious situation in which Ida's and Rufus' anger directly elicits the regeneration of the other characters in the novel while at the same time leading to their own demoralisation. Rufus commits suicide apparently because he is consumed by fury and self-pity, and Ida herself degenerates towards the end of the novel into a whining, self-conscious adolescent unduly intent on explaining away the moral compromises she is compelled to make in order to survive. The point to be made in this regard is that the function of anger in this novel is a curious one. It is not that the rage in *Another Country* is out of place, or that it is exaggerated (a point that not a few critics have failed to note)[6] but rather that Baldwin unconsciously appears to imply through his fictional situations that while anger might conceivably be the instrument of regeneration in its *object*, it inevitably consumes and destroys its subject. We shall see later how this arbitrary structure led to certain fundamental confusions that made *Another Country* a powerfully conceived but less than expertly executed work of fiction.

One of the intriguing indications of Baldwin's ambition in *Another Country* is the fact that Rufus, who is essentially the hero of this novel, dies quite early in the story; yet it is this very fact of his physical disappearance from the scene that provides for the novel the single most important organising principle that holds all the other episodes together. With the possible exception of Richard Silenski, who is presumably too far gone in obtuseness and egocentricity to learn anything from his experience, all the other major characters, Vivaldo, Eric, Cass and Ida, are profoundly affected by his life and death. Vivaldo, a would-be writer labouring painfully under the heavy burden of racial guilt, achieves a certain limited resolution of his confusions through his sense of betrayal of this black Christ; Eric's final reconciliation with his bisexuality is achieved through recognition of the vital significance of his brief but crucial affair with Rufus, an affair that is later extended into his life with Yves;[7] Cass Silenski finds whatever maturity she gains through her confrontation with Eric and Ida, both of whom have been profoundly influenced by Rufus, and Ida herself, the black and awesomely beautiful nemesis of this novel, inherits from her brother's death both her anger and whatever insight she finally achieves into the true nature of her dispossession. But to say that Rufus is the hero of this novel needs qualification, and it is in this qualification that we shall point out one of the major weaknesses of this novel. In precise terms, Rufus is more of an influence than a character, an ethereal emanation rather than a concretely delineated personality. It is true that we are given an actual description of the beginnings of his relationship with Leona, that once in a while we are offered snatches of his embittered conversations with Vivaldo, but beyond this much of what we are given is vague history of the deterministic sort, and Baldwin appears to have assumed, wrongly in our opinion, that merely to assert that Rufus was 'one of the fallen' was an effective substitute for actual presentation of detail. Consider, for instance, the passage in which we see Rufus standing, lonely and desperate, on Seventh Avenue:

Beneath them Rufus walked, one of the fallen, for the weight of this city was murderous—one of those who had been crushed on the day, which was every day, these towers fell. Entirely alone, and dying of it, he was part of an unprecedented multitude. There were boys and girls drinking coffee at the drugstore counters who were held back from his condition by barriers as perishable as their dwindling cigarettes. They could scarcely bear their knowledge, nor would they have borne the sight of Rufus, but they knew why he was in the streets tonight, why he rode subways all night long, why his stomach growled, why his hair was nappy, his armpits funky, his pants and shoes too thin, and why he did not dare to stop and take a leak.[8]

There is no doubt that the passage above is moving in its evocation of suffering and alienation in the midst of human indifference, but it tells us much less about Rufus than it does about his fellow travellers in despair and about the impersonal and vicious city in which he lives and dies. Since the opening pages of the novel are meant apparently to prepare us for his suicide, we are conditioned to expect a little more information regarding his predicament. In other words, we are not at all persuaded that there is an inevitable connection between the viciousness of his environment and his suicidal choice. It is not that we leave the novel without some idea of the nature of Rufus' predicament; he is black, and therefore dispossessed; he has had a love relationship with a white woman that ends in tragedy because, we presume, of the racist culture in which they are compelled to live. But it needs also to be observed that these are presumptions that derive from our idea of the author's intention in this novel but lack the kind of specificness that could lead to the clear conclusion that Rufus' suicide is historically determined—the consequence, that is, of his colour. For, as Rufus is himself aware, his loneliness is by no means unique:

> He had often thought of his loneliness, for example, as a condition which testified to his superiority. But people who were not superior were, nevertheless, extremely lonely—and unable to break out of their solitude precisely because they had no equipment with which to enter it. His own loneliness, magnified so many million times, made the night air colder. He remembered to what excesses, into what traps and nightmares, his loneliness had driven him, and he wondered where such a violent emptiness might drive an entire city.[9]

Here we have a useful example of part of the confusion in *Another Country*. On the one hand, it is in the nature of the story itself that we accept that Rufus' tragedy is the direct result of racist prejudice, his life a dramatic presentation of that stultification that springs from social malice. But on the other hand we note that loneliness, one of the tragic symptoms of his peculiar condition, is a malaise that infects the life of an 'entire city,' no less, in fact, than a 'universal condition.' One consequence of this confusion of a historically determined, with an existential, despair, then, is that contrary to what we must presume was the author's intention, Rufus' tragic end becomes not clearly inevitable, but quite possibly the result, if not of personal inadequacy, at least of some curious sort of existential choice. And here it is that we are confronted with a fundamental problem of elucidation in *Another Country*. Is Rufus the peculiar victim of a callous world, or is he primarily a weak-minded young man who falls victim to his own lack of vital purpose? Is Baldwin here concerned to dramatize the mortal effects of racism, or is he mainly intent on presenting the existential predicament of a single individual?

A second consideration has to do with the nature and effects of Rufus' rage. That he is angry is clear, and that there is very little he can do to alleviate his anger is also true. And at this point it may then be supposed that Baldwin here intended to suggest to us that the man who is a victim of racism has little recourse at his disposal *but to be angry and die*—a clearly false reading, both because Rufus' particular response is by no means generic, and also because those characters in the novel who may be supposed to be the objects of Rufus' anger, who appear to themselves to have little choice but to indulge in their sense of communal guilt (Richard Silenski is again an exception here) do in fact gain some measure at least of understanding of the nature of Rufus' despair. It is perfectly conceivable that one may be so angry as to take his own life, but it would clearly be false to suggest that such a choice is inevitable. And if this is so, it is reasonable to suggest that the confusion here between causes and their effects contributes to the vagueness that attends the political concerns of this novel. Those who believe that it is foolish to talk about a writer's intentions will no doubt object that we are here presuming a specific intention in the author's mind that by its very nature defies clear validation. Yet whatever the theoretical worth of this objection—and it is by no means certain that one is obliged to take it seriously anymore—it seems quite sensible to suggest that one of the fundamental intentions in *Another Country* is to dramatize in as powerful a manner as possible the evils of racial prejudice; and if this is so, it seems to us quite legitimate to examine the manner in which this intention is sustained in characterization.

In view of this confusion or ambiguity in the author's presentation of Rufus, it is fascinating to consider the quite graphic effect and influence he nevertheless has on the other characters in the novel. We suggested earlier that Rufus is in some vague way construed as a Christ-like figure, the unrecognised and uncelebrated prophet of a new religion.[10] But he does not teach any new doctrine, neither does he consciously surround himself with any disciples. He departs the world with a curse on his lips, and the only bequest he leaves behind is the memory of his pain and suffering. It is doubtless part of Baldwin's ironic comment on his world that in his life Rufus does not appear to be a significant being, does not appear to mean anything to anybody, whereas in his death he exercises a degree of influence on the lives of those who knew him that is altogether out of proportion to the seriousness or concern with which they take him while he is with them. The issue of betrayal is, one suspects, an important one in this novel, though it is difficult to capture the precise specifics of the matter. Perhaps what matters most is that both Vivaldo, Cass and Ida *believe* they betrayed Rufus. Vivaldo, for one, is so disturbed by this belief that he appears determined to expiate his sin by falling in love with Rufus' sister Ida. He is a well-intentioned young man, kind, considerate, and determined to be friends with Rufus. But the logic of the story appears to insist that we see him as inherently inhibited by the fact of his colour from giving fully of himself. Up till the time Rufus dies, his awareness of Rufus' pain and suffering appears to be limited to the insight that suffering is universal, a limitation that presumably leads to his failure to rescue Rufus in his time of critical need. Even after Rufus' death, we see him in his remorse striving desperately to hold on to the only certainties he knows of:

> I knew I failed him but I loved him too, and nobody there wanted to know that. I kept thinking. They're colored and I'm white but the same things have happened, really the same things, and how can I make them know that? [11]

The irony of the situation lies, of course, in Vivaldo's ingenuous pique at this point. He has had to live through almost as much suffering as Rufus—he is the son of impoverished Italian immigrants—and on a certain level it is difficult to draw much distinction between his and Rufus' dispossession. But in a practical sense, and as Cass rather pointedly instructs him, it is in the *causes* of his discontent and the limited possibilities he has for alleviating them that we must discover the crucial uniqueness of Rufus' tragic dilemma. Vivaldo is white, Rufus black, and that, in a racist culture, is the most poignant reality. Ultimately, then, his failure to perceive the complex anatomy of Rufus' pain leads to his betrayal of the latter. It is not that he is deliberately capricious, but there is something approaching dark comedy in the manner in which, on the night of Rufus' suicide, Vivaldo feels quite confident he has done all that any man may do for a friend in need, having fed and bought him drinks (and even offered him a woman to go home with). Rufus leaves him and his girl friend at the bar and walks away, never to be seen alive again, and Vivaldo's subsequent remorse is exactly in proportion to his earlier self-congratulation and exuberance at having rescued a friend from his misery. It is, too, in the context of this feeling of remorse that we may surmise that, after his conversation with Cass, Vivaldo quite makes up his mind to become Ida's lackey. Certainly there is that element of masochism in his relations with Ida which attests to his determination to bear all manner of contempt and injury in expiation, as it were, for his betrayal of Ida's brother.

Action is, in this novel, clearly presumed to be intricately linked to thought to a greater extent than we notice in Baldwin's earlier novels, but on a much deeper level it is the mental perspective that is of primary significance. Just as Vivaldo's shallowness of perception manifests itself in his betrayal of Rufus, so also does his subsequent understanding of the true distinction between his and Rufus' pain lead to his forebearance with Ida. The new country which Baldwin postulates in this novel is not a world of recognisably distinctive phenomena, but a country of the mind. There is in it no utopian absence of suffering and despair. It is a cold, sombre region, and indeed, to the extent that the pain of this new world is introverted, unshared and focused on the self, it is all the more intense and near insupportable. What distinguishes this new world from the one Baldwin renounces is not therefore a surfeit of happiness, but a profound recognition and acceptance of the tragedy of life.[12]

One of the more subtle situations in the novel derives from the consideration that the author sets Cass up as the one who gives Vivaldo his first lesson in the rules that regulate membership in this new communion of beings. On the one hand she is a rather improbable teacher to Vivaldo. A reasonably happy housewife with an adoring husband, she has lived most of her life within the shelter of privileged birth and colour. Her excursion into the underworld of racial prejudice and social squalor is relatively brief and, while Rufus lives, whatever intimations she may have of the inadequacies of her life are effectively contained by her concern for her family. But after Rufus' death, once she meets Ida and discovers Eric's battle to retain a semblance at least of personal integrity in a chaotic world, her composure quickly melts away, and she begins to recognise that the meaning of life goes quite beyond the confines of her genteel and rather uneventful life with her husband Richard. But it needs to be emphasized that if Cass does aspire to membership in Baldwin's new country, it is only in a provisional sense, in terms, that is, of her discovery that Rufus, Vivaldo and Eric belong to a world whose reality is more desperate and harrowing than the one she inhabits. Her link to Eric's world is rather one of sympathy than of commitment. In her brief flirtation with the latter, she attests to an ability to understand what men like Rufus and Eric must suffer, but she cannot permanently remain in this world. Her final break with Eric is explainable partly in terms of dramatic necessity —the citizens of Baldwin's new world are basically rootless men for whom a break with the old world is relatively easy, whereas Cass' ties to the old world are not sufficiently tenuous or painful to justify a complete break; but what is more significant is that her ambiguous ties to this world are bound to be superficial, because it is essentially a man's world. It is a man's world because the homosexual principle operates in it, and because the permanent presence in it of women is likely to lead to a corruption of the homosexual ideal of manly affection. While Rufus, Eric and Vivaldo are natural members of this risky utopia, Cass and Ida may only be temporarily initiated into it. In Ida's case, of course, her colour and her blood relationship to the somewhat unwitting founder of this new faith give her an edge over Cass. Again, in terms of the pain and unending despair of her life, Ida is potentially ideal as an initiate—she, too, has very tenuous ties with the old world and is just as dispossessed as the male members of this new world—but ultimately her suffering and humiliation are made out to be merely statistical, quantitative. Even at the end of the story, when she has gone through the limits of degradation with Ellis, it is her self-pity that comes out more strongly than her ability to transcend the shame of her life and accept herself (but one could easily say the same thing of her brother—which leads one to the suspicion that the determination of citizenship in this new world is just as arbitrary as it is in the old world, a painful thought). At this critical point in her life it is clear that it requires the heroic forebearance and understanding of a now regenerate Vivaldo to pull her across the abyss of despair, precisely the kind of service that would quite literally have saved Rufus from the bridge. And in this context it is part of Baldwin's success in this novel that Vivaldo's final acceptance of Ida is not coated with undue sentimentality. For one thing, that Ida should finally seek forgiveness from a member of that race which she formerly despised could become an unjustifiable *tour de force* if ineptly handled, but the rendering of the scene flows with a degree of complexity of emotions that both indicates Vivaldo's growing regeneration and leads one to recognise Baldwin's own control of his material at this point. Ida's 'confiteor hominem,' though perfectly plausible, is not a little surprising, but it is equally fitting that there should be nothing unduly definitive about Vivaldo's priestlike role—he is, in fact, at odds to discover the most appropriate and honest response to her confession:

He was afraid to go near her, he was afraid to touch her, it was almost as though she had told him that she had been infected with the plague. His arms trembled with his revulsion, and every act of the body seemed unimaginably vile. And yet, at the same

time, as he stood helpless and stupid in the kitchen . . . his heart
began to beat with a newer, stonier anguish, which destroyed the
distance called pity and placed him, very nearly, in her body . . .
He went to her, resigned and tender and helpless, her sobs seem-
ing to make his belly sore.[13]

If Vivaldo has to make this spiritual journey in order to accept Ida
for what she is, it is well to remember that at this point Ida's pristine rage has long been dissipated, her self-assurance gone, and in
the true tradition of the neophyte, the seeker after virtue, it is precisely at the moment she divests herself of all the props that had
seemed to her so necessary that she truly becomes a candidate for
initiation.

If Vivaldo, Cass and Ida achieve their differing levels of maturity
within the dramatic movement of the novel, within its time span,
Eric is the one figure whose fixed and immovable compassion appears to precede the story itself. In many ways Rufus' alter ego, he
reminds one of what the former might have become had he lived.
Where Rufus is the Christ-figure whose martyrdom is necessary for
the birth of a new religion, Eric is the Pauline apostle through
whom the gospel is disseminated. That he extricates his sense of
inner peace from his life with Rufus is made quite explicit in the
story. It is through the risk, the danger and the complicated passions of this relationship that he achieves that perspective that later
bears him through the desperate ambiguities of life.[14] And just as
Rufus' benign influence is oddly paradoxical, so also does Eric
affect the lives of those he intimately meets without apparently
trying. Even Ida in her days of anger finds it not a little difficult to
dislike him. His homosexuality is a cross he has to bear through
life, but rather than deny it as Vivaldo tries, and fails to do, he
learns, by the time he returns to New York, to accept it, and it is
precisely because of his ability to come to terms with himself that
he becomes so powerful an influence on his friends. For Vivaldo he
is the teacher who reveals the truth that to love a fellow man need
not be an act of shameful degradation; for Cass Silenski he is the
compassionate friend with whom adultery becomes less a sin than a
veritable journey of self-discovery, and even Ida, the embattled

Fury of the novel, watches her passionate contempt dissolve as she finds she has little choice but to be friends with Eric.

Eric is the true apostle and inheritor of that country founded upon the tragedy of Rufus' life and suicide, but though his own character is delineated effectively enough, we are not at all persuaded that the contours of the new world to which his life is presumed to be committed, are sufficiently distinguished to bear the burden of Baldwin's conceptual dream. Vivaldo, Eric, Cass, and Ida to a lesser degree, may through Rufus' death and by the extension of his influence through Eric, have come to the realisation that to be truly alive is to be prepared to risk everything, that to love is to be willing to give entirely of oneself; they may, through painful confrontation with self, have achieved a spiritual regeneration that could conceivably attain them the state of grace, but the quite fundamental charge must still be made that their spiritual rebirth, as Eldridge Cleaver was quick to remark not so long ago, appears ultimately to be little more than a gesture of transcendence, significant in and of itself, but hardly sufficiently weighty to justify the supposition that they therefore belong to a *different* 'country.' Even if we were to suppose that theirs is a Marcusean leap[15]—a leap that is consummated in spite of the contradictions and obstacles inherent in the fact that they still live with us—even if we were to suppose that theirs is a transformation that is significant primarily in a spiritual sense—and the evidence does point to this supposition—it still does not appear to us that there is a sufficiently significant qualitative difference between the nature of their lives and ours. The real world of Baldwin's novel, the world of which New York is a microcosm, is presented, it must be admitted, with sufficient and imaginative intensity. Baldwin is often at his best when describing the squalor of Harlem, the desperate and suicidal conviviality of the Village, and his evocation of the impersonality of the city at night is a moving one. Furthermore, very few can read *Another Country* and fail to be affected by the oppressive intensity of the fury of this novel, by Ida's anger, or by the homicidal passions of Vivaldo's gigantic adversary in the red districts of Harlem. The *geography* of the real world of Baldwin's denunciations is unmistakably clear in this novel, and it would perhaps have been a much better novel had he left it at that. But in seeking to postulate a qualitatively superior world, an eternal city of which Eric and Vivaldo would be plausible citizens, Baldwin appears to have overlooked the quite serious consideration that the most probable dwelling place for gods is Elysium, not New York, and that his rather tortured saints had the clear choice therefore either to transport themselves, both spiritually and physically, from our real squalid world, or be seen to make the effort, at least, to bring their benign influence to bear upon their environment. As it turned out, they appear to have been unaware of either choice, and consequently, despite their apparent inner certainty of purpose (Eric's especially), they move around in an alienated and merely hypothetically 'new' world, a world of the mind in which nothing seemed to matter more than the individual's ability to convince himself that his own suffering had ensured that his life would overflow with fulfilment. Ironically, this curious hiatus between perception and action derives precisely from the concreteness of Baldwin's delineation of the actual world which his saints seek to escape from, for if we are being made to accept their ultimate difference from us on an allegorical plane, the presentation of the world from which they seek to withdraw is much too solid, much too insistently real to warrant such an allegorical interpretation.

In a sense, of course, the confusion here referred to is basically only a particularization of a perennial problem of method that most builders of utopia have to contend with: either they present us with a new world that merely implies its opposite, in which case they are often driven by some inner logic to dwell in the realms of sheer fantasy, or they offer us a concrete enough description both of the world they denounce and the one they embrace and invoke into being, in which case the fiction is likely to be clumsy and unwieldy. But Baldwin, in *Another Country*, appears to have recognised a third but hardly more effective choice, namely, the concretization of the unacceptable world and the invocation of a new world largely by implication. In this regard, then, the problem in this novel is a much larger one than appears to be implied in Cleaver's now famous but rather hasty verdict.[16] What we are faced with here goes quite beyond questions of ideology or political wisdom. It has ultimately to do with the artist's control over the material he voluntarily selects for his works. If Baldwin's saints exist in a vacuum, the reservation needs to be made that this is not for want of a clearly delineated geography of racial malevolence and moral squalor in the real world. If, as Cleaver rightly points out (though for rather curious reasons) Rufus is a pathetically poor guide to the socio-political foundations of the evil in the world of Baldwin's denunciations, one can hardly leave the novel unaffected by Ida's furious quest for vengeance or by the near anthropomorphic wickedness of 'the city' itself. Though the structural links are undoubtedly weak, it seems legitimate to suggest that Ida's anger, if not Rufus' despair, does have its roots in a visible fictional reality. And though the effectiveness of *Another Country* as a novel is vitiated by the absence of a more comprehensive structural link between the responses of individual characters and the social forces that motivate them, these characters finally appear to exist in a vacuum not because we fail to see the world from which they seek to escape, but because we cannot see the world to which they choose to run. The 'other country' of Baldwin's imagination is, in short, a nebulous, amorphous world that seems to exist only in the minds of his characters and is largely invisible to us. The invocation of this nebulous world was, moreover, not unlike the celestial dreams of that church which Baldwin had broken away from so many years before *Another Country* was published, and this similarity is in itself sufficient indication that he had not entirely divorced his vision from the religious imagination of his earlier novels.

A final evaluation of the measure of Baldwin's success in this novel has to do essentially with questions of intention and subsequent achievement. It is legitimate to suggest that after *Go Tell* and *Giovanni's Room*, he had begun to recognise that an exclusively theological definition of man was conceptually inadequate, even though one could employ it as a plausible thematic centre to an effective work of art. *Another Country* was Baldwin's testament to the growing comprehensiveness of his vision of life, to his nascent recognition that it is fanciful to insist on spiritual realities and apocryphal dreads to the exclusion of the socio-political ambience of man's life. The intention and the recognition were in themselves, therefore, a welcome indication of his growing maturity, of his awareness that excellence of form alone was an inadequate index of greatness in art, if it did not appear as the embodiment of meaningful as well as communicable content. In the case of Baldwin, at any rate, it needs to be emphasized that the issue was not whether or not he possessed a 'correct' ideology; his was not a political predicament, though one may question his political insights. He was not obliged to attest to a 'revolutionary' consciousness—one does not have to do this to bear witness to the fulness of life—but neither was it expected that he should become the permanent historian of a real but nonetheless dissociated sensibility.

It is plausible to suggest that Baldwin had come to this realisation by the time *Another Country* was written, but the mere recognition of the need for a comprehensive vision was clearly not quite enough; he had to demonstrate this in practice, and it is in the light of this latter consideration that this novel is one whose success is episodic, disintegrated, and whose failure lies essentially in the implausibility of the total vision, the result of an imperfectly structured tale. Herein, then, lies the fundamental paradox of Baldwin's development as a writer. So long as he testified to a rarefied, highly private theological vision, he was capable of producing a novel whose success lay, not in its parts, but in its total effect. But once he began to move toward a more public vision, the psychic effort demanded by this radical change appears to have led to an unfortunate attenuation of his formal artistic talent. In this novel we are offered intimations of this predicament, but it is in his latest novel, *Tell Me How Long the Train's Been Gone*, that we are likely to find a clearer dramatization of this dilemma.

Notes to Chapter Five

1. Baldwin, *The Amen Corner*, Dial, 1968, p. xv
2. ibid.

3. Between *Giovanni's Room* and *Another Country*, Baldwin had published two other books, *The Amen Corner*, a play, and *Notes of a Native Son*, his first collection of essays. But even in these works he seemed to have been more concerned with exploring his own private history than he was in *Go Tell*

4. Baldwin, Notes for *Amen Corner*, p. xv

5. Eckman, op. cit., pp. 123–24

6. See Mike Thelwell, 'Another Country: Baldwin's New York Novel' in C. E. Bigsby, ed., *The Black American Writer: Vol. II, Fiction*, Florida, Everett Edwards, 1969, p. 182 passim

7. We are in fact specifically told that Yves' resemblance to Rufus is the secret of his attraction for Eric. Baldwin, *Another Country*, Corgi, 1965, p. 149

8. ibid., p. 3

9. ibid., pp. 47–48

10. The allusion to christian mythology is not really that far-fetched. Consider, e.g., (i) Rufus' period of wandering in the urban wilderness (ii) his 'last supper' with Vivaldo, and the final sharing of wine with Vivaldo, Richard and Cass, p. 56 ff (iii) the 'betrayal' by Vivaldo, p. 65, and (iv) Rufus' cry from the bridge that serves as his cross, p. 69

11. Baldwin, *Another Country*, p. 89

12. See C. B. Cox and A. R. Jones, 'After the Tranquilized Fifties: Notes on Sylvia Plath and James Baldwin,' *Critical Quarterly*, Vol. 6, No. 2, June 1964, pp. 116–17

13. Baldwin, *Another Country*, p. 332

14. ibid., pp. 149–50, 266 passim

15. See Herbert Marcuse, 'A Reply to Lucien Goldman,' *Partisan Review*, Vol. xxxviii, No. 4, Winter 1971–72, esp. p. 400

16. Eldridge Cleaver, *Soul on Ice*, McGraw-Hill, 1968, p. 109

Six

The Agony of Blackness

I

One of the conditions of black art in the United States has always been that the individual writer was compelled, whether he liked it or not, to attempt to come to terms with his colour, and with the often quite frightful implications of this fact. It took a long and prolonged history of sometimes grandiosely trivial commentary in the fields of sociology and political science before it began to be grudgingly admitted, if only for negative reasons, that the black condition could not, in its essence, usefully be seen as being analogous to that of other 'minority' groups in the country; but we would not be overstating the case if we observed that an admission that so significantly helped in the clarification of the problems of analysis in various other disciplines is yet to be made in the discipline of criticism. It is not, of course, that critics have not, in the main, been perceptive enough to discover some of the specific characteristics of 'Negro Literature', but the discovery has itself most often been accompanied by a curious form of unease, demonstrated either in the insistence that an unabashed meditation upon the nature of blackness constitutes an inevitable limitation on artistic competence, or in the equally mystifying view that whatever is unique in Black Literature is that also which binds it inextricably to fundamental trends in the American literary mainstream. The confusion that attends the serious discussion of Black Literature appears even more paradoxical when it is considered that critical presumptions that are taken for granted in regard of other writers become, in the case of black writers, the point of giddy and irrele-

103

vant contention. The analogy that is often bandied around in these discussions is invariably that of the writer of Jewish descent, and it is often implied, if not blandly stated, that the Jewish writer has achieved such a transcendence of his particular inheritance that what is significant in his works is no longer his sometimes unconscious evocations of 'ethnicity' but the more typically 'American', 'Western', or 'universal' themes of his writing. Such a view clearly overlooks the consideration that the *parvenu* urbanity and sophistication of Mailer's essays, for instance, are in themselves not of any great over-riding significance except in so far as they illustrate the tragi-comic efforts of a sensibility strenuously determined on being 'American' rather than Jewish. For all its brilliant insights and scintillating aphorisms, *The Armies of the Night* is quite forgettable as a historical document (or, for that matter, as a novel); the historian who searches its tumid pages for authentic history would be rewarded with little more than confusion and frustration. But it is, nevertheless, an important document, not, certainly, in the sense that it provides a reliable account of the spirit of the falsely euphoric sixties, but rather in the sense that it encapsulates the essence of the Jewish American's confrontation with the American Dream. Norman Mailer was in *The Armies of the Night* determined to convince us, not merely that he had arrived at the threshold of American (for which read Celtic, Anglo-Saxon or what you will) sophistication, but that his sensibility had been so thoroughly 'Anglicised' that he had in fact quite become the authentic custodian of that self-conscious, maverick conservatism which he appeared to see as the peculiar possession of the New England gentleman. How, otherwise, may one comprehend his possibly ironic but certainly implausible effort to legislate himself into Lowell's 'patrician' inheritance;[1] what, from a different perspective, would be the precise significance of his quarrel with Paul Goodman, his fellow sexologue, were we not to understand it as deriving, among other things, from an identical discomfiture over sexual morals, a discomfiture that was as much part of the 'Judaic' tradition as it was later to serve as a basic attraction between 'unemotional' Jew and 'rational' gentile, even of the Catholic species?

The point here is a trivial one, really, namely, that no manner of rhetorical or artistic posturing is likely to entirely invalidate the essence (mythic or immediate) of the writer's experience. If the critic chooses not to dwell upon the specific ethnicities in Mailer's "The White Negro," in Bellow's *Henderson the Rain King* (the hero of which novel appears to be a curiously updated version of Moses on the banks of the Red Sea) or in Kerouac's rather silly visions of the black and Hispanic sensibility, it is certainly not because these ethnic undercurrents have been entirely 'transcended'; rather, there appears to be an implicit, school-tie sort of pact between writer and critic that the latter may not dwell too strenuously on those aspects of meaning which the writer considers it insufficiently genteel, or embarassing to emphasize. And it is by virtue of these unspoken understandings that we are left with such fictional figures as the Pawnbroker, Hertzog and Portnoy who, we are told, are nothing if not symbols of a deculturized, universal predicament. But the black writer in America belongs, essentially, in a different category, partly because he has never had the privilege of being signatory to this pact, and partly also because he is not, in the main, nearly so willing that his particular condition be swallowed up by that inscrutably white whale of universality. In a very fundamental sense, therefore, his exclusion from this genteel pact between writer and critic (a situation that renders the claim that he belongs inevitably to the mainstream of American letters downright capricious) and the insistent immediacy of his particular condition constitute, then, the outer limits of his agony, and few black writers here have exemplified this agony as Baldwin has. We have seen how, in *Another Country*, his desperate search for some mitigation of this agony led to the postulation of an implausible and imperfectly conceived utopian Eden that was by its very nature inadequate to deal with the social problems that were meant to justify it. But when viewed from the perspective of literary history, it may reasonably be argued that Baldwin's conceptual problem in *Another Country* was by no means unique. If it is admitted that an abiding theme in Black Literature in America, as in Black history in general, has always been a search for resolution of a complex fate that takes its basic source from the fact of colour, it becomes clear that Baldwin's resolutions in *Another Country* are no more quaint, no less intelligible than the resolutions offered by writers like DuBois, Garvey, or McKay. Indeed, with respect to Black Literature in particular, the significance and vitality of this literature derives not so much from the objective 'correctness' or appropriateness of the specific resolutions offered as from the attempt itself, from our ability to observe the processes of thought and feeling that lead the characters in this literature to a particular choice. In other words, one need not accept either as sufficient or inevitable the choices that Bigger Thomas, the Invisible Man, or Max Reddick (the hero of John A. Williams' *The Man Who Cried I Am*) makes in order to be deeply moved by the agonised attempts of these characters to resolve their predicament. Black Literature may, and does often suggest alternative modes both of perception and of resolution, but when it is significant, its importance seldom derives from the objective sufficiency of whatever 'ultimate' answers it may provide for the riddles of Blackness. While it is, therefore, quite legitimate to identify the conceptual and other limitations of Baldwin's works, it must also be borne in mind that they are by no means limited to him, and a brief historical survey of the development of Black Literature in America will illustrate this conclusion.

II

Assuming that the folk origins of this literature derive more immediately from the Spirituals and Slave Songs, it is important to remember that while they may have served as philosophical consolations, as repositories of folk experience, they did not, in the main, constitute a blueprint or practical guide to action. They did have a significant and all-important function, but they do not, in their complex totality, constitute a modern *Georgics*. And the longstanding controversy over the meaning and function of the Blues and Spirituals notwithstanding, it may reasonably be suggested, as Ellison has argued, that their function was essentially therapeutic, psychological, rather than practical. If we must search, then, for the historical antecedents, *in America*, of Ron Karenga's advocacy of that art that is 'functional, collective, and committing', we obviously will not find them in the Blues or Spirituals;[2] and neither, for that matter, are we likely to discover any direct intimations of this conception of art in Black Literature of the Romantic period. The black writers of the late eighteenth and early nineteenth centuries were motivated in their art less by a desire to celebrate their sense of blackness than by a need they felt to assert their common humanity. As Ruth Miller has observed, such writers as Phylis Wheatley, Martin Delaney, James Whitfield, George Horton and Frances Harper were, no doubt, aware of the contradictions of their situation, but it was precisely because of this awareness that they felt obliged to demonstrate that they belonged, with the white writers of the period, in the same general tradition.[3] Phylis Wheatley's elaborately grandiose elegiacs are hardly distinguishable from those of the less important poets of the eighteenth century, and George Horton's invocations of liberty, though they obviously take their source from a real and painful experience, appear in the end to be overly contrived and stylised, unintentionally denoting false and spurious emotion:

> Say unto foul oppression, Cease:
> Ye tyrants rage no more
> And let the joyful trump of peace,
> Now bid the vassal soar.

> Soar on the pinions of the dove
> Which long has cooed for thee,
> And breathed her notes from Afric's grove,
> The sound of Liberty.[4]

As an attempt to resolve an immediate and pressing problem, this tedious verse-making was, of course, an occasionally useful weapon for achieving freedom, as witness the more fortunate career of Phylis Wheatley, and in a quite fundamental sense the assumption that the black man belonged to a common humanity with his white compatriots was a tragically ironic comment on a typical faith of the Romantic era. Those who believed in the unity of the universe, of man, nature and inanimate matter, could hardly have failed to recognise the hideous paradox in their simultaneous belief in the bestiality of the black man, and since we must assume that the black writers of the period were aware of this paradox, one may understand why they often chose to believe that the path to freedom lay in their ability to ape the literary caprices of their slave masters. Understandable as their choice is, it should, however, be remarked that a tragic corollary of this insistence on their common humanity was the tendency to de-emphasize, if not to deny, their blackness. It was not that they uniformly avoided the subject of black life and history, but, as in the case of Martin Delaney's *Blake*, the subject matter was itself often the means, merely, by which the agonised writer sought to establish the superiority of his sensibility over that of his lowly and 'primitive' fellows. Whether the hero was an 'educated' ex-slave, a blandly congenial farmhand, or a 'tragic mulatto', the writer's sympathies often suggested a preference for those of his characters who had managed, or were striving to attain a semblance of 'civilized' behavior. At the point, therefore, at which he was constrained to equate 'civilization' with a fledgling Euro-American culture, and to study its cultivation as a means of achieving his own liberation, he became in fact an ironic accessory to the exacerbation of that Romantic paradox that was to have a crucial impact on the subsequent achievements of later black writers.

From the vantage point of hindsight, it can hardly now be doubted that Paul Lawrence Dunbar's folk realism was in large part a reaction to this Romantic, assimilationist approach to black art. That his dialect poems were often more technically competent and more representative of his feelings than his more formal poetry was no accident. Despite the commercial, promotional considerations that doubtless influenced his choice, the theoretical presuppositions that led to it were clearly more significant. As in the case of the writers of the earlier period, prevalent literary attitudes contributed, of course, to this choice. The turn of the century was the age of the Realist-Naturalists, an age in which American writers were, in general, becoming much less disposed to endorse the stylized artificialities of the late Romantics. But to employ, in formal art, the folk language of black people was in fact to insist, not on the common inheritance of blacks and whites, but primarily on the uniqueness of black life. From the perspective of black intellectual history, therefore, Dunbar's choice was a crucial departure, one that was to have far-reaching effects in the black world, both in Africa and the United States. His pioneering work provided the theoretical justification for much of the achievement of the Harlem Renaissance, and the Renaissance was in turn to influence later the evolution of the African philosophy of Negritude.

A closer examination of Dunbar's decision to write and publish dialect poems suggests, however, that his influence was an extremely ambiguous one. To the extent that Booker T. Washington, DuBois, and Claude McKay may be seen to have derived part, at least, of the justification for their own thoughts from Dunbar's pioneering work,[5] it seems clear now that not all black writers and thinkers had the same views on the blessings of 'Realism'. For Washington, it seemed a 'realistic' approach to argue that blacks should relinquish the struggle for social and political freedom and work rather for economic self-sufficiency through vocational training. That there was implicit in this view a tragic sense of racial inferiority did not seem to matter much to him, so long as the proposal appeared eminently practical; and despite the formidable rigour of DuBois' own writings, it seems clear also that in his search for 'realistic' solutions, he could not entirely avoid the temptation of superimposing an elitist, anti-populist advocacy over his celebrations of racial pride. But in spite, however, of their well-publicised disagreements over matters of policy, it would appear that both Washington and DuBois were motivated by an identical constraint to discover some 'realistic' principle of action or thought that would mitigate, if not entirely remove the sources of their racial discontent. Where Washington was more populist and democratic, DuBois tended to be rather elitist in his thought. Where Washington was more concerned to elevate through discipline and low-level vocational training the down-trodden men of the rural backwaters, DuBois seemed more determined to testify to the sophistication and urbanity of a small minority of black professionals in the cities. In this respect the affinities between Washington and Marcus Garvey do provide some illumination on DuBois' abhorrence of the former's ideas.

But from the perspective of the history of ideas, the specifics of the disagreements between Washington and DuBois encompass a historic dichotomy in black American thought between the 'communitarian' and the elitist-individualist principles. And in spite of their differences, the failure of both men lay primarily in their apparent inability to recognise that their positions were quite capable of reconciliation, at least in theory. It was to be left to the younger writers of the Renaissance (and this is part of their achievement) to attempt a synthesis of this dichotomy, and McKay's poetry is a useful illustration of this observation. If Washington and DuBois appeared in their controversy to suggest that their positions were essentially incompatible, McKay managed in his poetry often to suggest that it was quite possible for a sense both of community and of individual worth to cohabit the same mind. The ostensible organising principle in much of his poetry is an often exquisitely expressed fury, a palpable rage against social discrimination and injustice. The subject of his poems is, in other words, one that derives from a communal sense of dispossession, but the specific resolutions that emanate from this communal sense, are, quite often, individualistic in the extreme. Though the mood of his famous poem, 'If We Must Die,' precedes the flowering of the existentialist sensibility in Western literature, the counsels of desperate confrontation which it embodies are in fact 'suicidal' in the sense that Camus would have understood the term. McKay, in this poem, appears to begin with the negative presupposition that 'we must die,' and what subsequently matters is not, apparently, that our death might become an instrument, a means of resolving the racial dilemma, but that we might, by the manner, the dignity and the courage of our dying, attest to a nobility that the oppressor seems determined to deny. Hemingway would no doubt have approved of this impassioned call to dignified death, and if Winston Churchill found this poem quite appropriate for his crusade against fascism, he must either have been unconvinced of the world's ability to defeat Hitler, or he pitifully misunderstood the tension in this poem between a call to communal effort and an essentially suicidal and pessimistic search for individual self-justification. The above analysis of McKay's poem is, of course, more useful as description than as judgment, for when seen in its proper historical perspective, it seems clear that the poet's conceptual achievement in this poem was his ability to contain within the same sonnet the two principles of community and individuality which, in the hands of his predecessors, appeared to be impossible of synthesis.

The celebration of blackness which Dunbar had begun with his dialect poems became, in the hands of Claude McKay a most complex literary technique. But objective historical analysis would suggest that the particular resolutions of the agony of blackness which McKay offered in his poems were just as inadequate as Booker T. Washington's more obvious counsels of racial humility. In his poem, 'The Harlem Dancer,' for instance, the celebration of the beauty and nobility of black womanhood is underscored by what we see as a self-conscious and arbitrary dissociation of the poet's sensibility from the more general vulgarity and spiritual blindness of the dancer's audience.[6] The identity of the audience is itself ambiguous enough, and it is therefore difficult to attribute to the poet any clear intention to emphasize (assuming the audience is white) that pitiful lack of sympathy and a proper awareness of the spiritual values of 'dance' which a black audience would presumably have clearly demonstrated. Since such a cultural reading of the poem would be quite misleading, it seems reasonable to suggest that the dancer is here something of a surrogate for the poet, a personality whose assurance of superiority has made a transcendence of material pain possible. And if this is indeed the case, we would not be overstating the case if we argued that this dissociation, this detachment, was more akin to DuBois' elitist attitudes than to Washington's less glamorous proposals. With respect to McKay, however, an extenuating consideration would be that he was not alone in this possession of a merely nominal political consciousness. For all their hilarious rituals of racial celebration, a good many of the black writers of the Twenties appear to have been incapable of achieving that conceptual link between art and politics that was to become the forte of later writers, such as LeRoi Jones and Ed Bullins. It was not that they excluded socio-political issues from their writings, as McKay's own furious political rage clearly indicates, nor was it that the times were lacking in sufficiently catastrophic crises and upheavals; but to the extent that they were influenced by prevalent literary attitudes, Jean Toomer's record suggests that the black writers of this period could hardly have failed to be tempted, despite their more immediate predicament, by the alienated sensibility that motivated Malcolm Cowley's exiles.

The most important black thinker of the Renaissance who provided a specifically political interpretation of the agony of blackness was, of course, Marcus Garvey. More than Washington's or DuBois', his was the one sensibility at the time that was at once theoretical, programmatic and organisational. He appears to have had little use for the existentialist 'if we must die' sophistications of McKay (though it is necessary to remark, also, that the animosity was quite mutual) nor does the record suggest that he was particularly attracted either to Washington's unprepossessing pragmatisms (though the latter influenced his thoughts quite profoundly) or to DuBois' urbane intellectualisms. But ultimately the processes of reasoning and experience that led to Garvey's choice were fundamentally no different from those that were later to lead to the utopian dream in Baldwin's *Another Country*. For both men a crucial assumption was that of the moral superiority of blackness, a superiority, however, that stood the danger of corruption in the land of their dispossession. Both men were motivated by a profound unwillingness to accept their condition as permanent and ineluctable, and both in their own way dreamt of some pristine Eden in which there would be neither pain nor racial injustice. But a more significant relationship between Baldwin's and Garvey's ideas—as between them and other black writers and thinkers—was that they all were driven by the need to discover a response, a resolution of their unbearable predicament. We must be careful, however, not to stress these relationships beyond the point where they cannot be supported by historical evidence. Garvey's vision was an essentially Mannichean one; for him there appeared to be no hesitations before what he saw as the need to divide the world into two moral absolutes: black was good, white bad, and the virtuous had no business truckling with those who had made their love of evil manifestly clear. Further, Garvey's ultimate dream, quaint as it appeared to many at the time, was a perfectly conceivable one (black men and women *had* once moved to Africa from here and resettled in their ancestral land) and one that was quite capable of realisation in practice. Baldwin's utopia in *Another Country* was, on the other hand, directed toward the resolution of the agony, viewed from a different perspective. His was a mythic search for therapeutic release, in the manner of the Spirituals and early Blues, unaccompanied by any programs or blueprints for social amelioration. But by far the most fundamental distinction between Garvey and Baldwin was precisely this, that where Garvey saw the black man's sojourn in America as a temporary, if vexatious irritation that must lead to a final return to Africa, Baldwin appears always to have worked from the presupposition that he and those like him were irretrievably bound to this country, and had no choice but to think of themselves as Americans.

On the face of it, a comparison between Garvey and Baldwin seems improbable and sophistical, especially since Garvey's was a much more bureaucratic mind than Baldwin's, yet an examination of their record suggests that neither of them was unimpeachable in their theoretical positions. Despite the practical programs with which it was surrounded, it can hardly now be denied that Garvey's Back to Africa Movement was buttressed upon a largely sentimentalised conception of Africa. His Africa was not, in essence, the Africa of the colonial Twenties; to the extent that he was seriously concerned with a return to the homeland (and the issue does, in our opinion, deserve further exploration) his Africa seemed sometimes to be a continent in which authentic history had come to a halt, presumably at the point where 'even the great poets of old sang in beautiful sonnets of the delight it afforded the gods to be in companionship with the Ethiopians.' When he consciously recognised the rape and degradation of the colonial era, it was often as though he saw these primarily as episodes in European, rather than in African history. (Odd as this may seem, both Garvey and European historians of the twentieth century appear to have been guilty of a complementary historical fallacy—where authentic African history seems for Garvey to have ended with the collapse of the great African civilisations, it begins, for many British historians, with the history of European activity in Africa.) His perception of the psychic effects of conquest and exploitation is hardly comparable in its depth to Frantz Fanon's; and he may therefore have underestimated the seriousness of the problems, cultural, social and political that his returning exiles would have had to face in Africa. To this extent, then, there was a degree of utopianism implicit in Garvey's thought (one that is perhaps illustrated in Yambo Ouloguem's controversial novel, *Bound to Violence*) that places Baldwin's own later ideas in a certain historical perspective, and at this point it would be profitable to examine in some detail the content of his response to the agony of blackness.

A fundamental idea in Baldwin's vision has always been that of man, and especially of the black man as a victim of 'history'. Whether this was expressed in theological (as in his earlier novels) or socio-political terms, the sporadic optimism of some of his writings never entirely conceals his basic belief that the black man is obliged to live as best he can through a tragic nightmare that is quite often not of his own making.[7] No doubt the apocalyptic vision he inherited from the fundamentalism of the Black Church contributed to the development of this idea, and the specific conditions of his birth and citizenship in America were hardly calculated to encourage in him any Whitmanesque celebrations of the promises of the New World. It does seem plausible however, to suggest that the most profound source of this belief appears to be Baldwin's meditation upon the nature of his relationship to Africa. He has never really, in his creative works, dwelt upon the meaning of his exile here, certainly not in the sustained manner in which either Melvin Tolson (in 'Dark symphony') or Robert Hayden (in 'Middle Passage') has employed this theme, but many of his essays are full of brief references to his African origins. And in this regard the single most crucial consideration appears to him to be the fact that, for various reasons, his ancestors found themselves on the American continent, and were compelled therefore to break, in time, all ties with their original homeland. Baldwin has never appeared to be unduly impressed by theories of cultural survivals in black America, and only in recent years has he shown any willingness to concede the possibility, at least, of a world view of blackness. More intrinsic to his thought has been the view that, by virtue of his transportation to the New World, the black man became as authentic (if not the most authentic) a citizen of this continent as any of the Pilgrim Fathers could claim to be. It was not that he adopted the theory of the melting pot, or of assimilation (indeed, a fundamental issue in his quarrel with Richard Wright's *Native Son* was precisely his conviction that Wright had failed in this novel to provide a sufficiently cogent account of black tradition and culture in America) but Baldwin appears quite early in his career to have made up his mind that a clear, definitive and ireversible rupture was established by the fact of Slavery and the Slave Trade, and consequently, the problem has been for him not one of re-establishing the black American's African ties (either through a desire to return from exile or through a deliberate cultivation, in America, of African consciousness) but of coming to terms with a condition that is at once immediate and permanent. It must be emphasized that Baldwin's conception of a permanent rupture from Africa did not and does not imply a desire for assimilation or integration, except in a very superficial sense. It is in fact one of his major contributions to the debate over the nature and meaning of blackness that he quite early in his career developed the theory of the black American as a 'link'—"the most shocking of all African contributions to Western cultural life"—between Africa and the West. His denunciations of Western culture are famous enough, but what is not often recognised in his equally determined refusal to lay claim to a usable African patrimony. And in spite of some of its rather obtuse and mystifying details, the main tenor of the justification he provides for this position is largely unexceptionable:

. . . the land of our fore-fathers' exile had been made, by that travail, our home. It may have been the popular impulse to keep us at the bottom of the perpetually shifting and bewildered populace; but we were, on the other hand, almost personally indispensable to each of them, simply because, without us, they could never have been certain, in such a confusion, where the bottom was; and nothing, in any case, could take away our title to the land which we, too, had purchased with our blood. This results in a psychology very different—at its best and at its worst—from the psychology which is produced by a sense of having been invaded and overrun, the sense of having no recourse whatever against oppression other than overthrowing the machinery of the oppressor. We had been dealing with, had been made and mangled by a different machinery altogether.[8]

The view herein expressed came a good many years before the flowering of the Civil Rights Movement and the later resurgence of black militancy, and the context in which it was expressed suggests that Baldwin had as yet not experienced that profound disillusionment that was to lead to the apocalyptic predictions of *The Fire Next Time* or the guarded advocacies of militant confrontation in *No Name in the Street*. Certainly, when in the same passage he claims that in contrast to the African predicament it had never been in the interest of black Americans to overthrow the machinery of oppression, or that what distinguished black Americans from 'non-American Negroes' was

. . . the banal and abruptly quite overwhelming fact that we had been born in a society, which, in a way quite inconceivable for Africans, and no longer real for Europeans, was open, and, in a way which has nothing to do with justice or injustice, free;

when he argues that he and his black compatriots had been born into a society 'in which nothing was fixed and we had therefore been born to a greater number of possibilities, wretched as these possibilities seemed at the instant of our birth,'[9] one can only conclude that in his desire to find justification for a perfectly legitimate sentiment, he had been tempted into a degree of naivety that was almost unbelievable.

Despite his unwillingness, however, to accept as given the hypothesis that there was any obvious, meaningful and unmediated link between the cultures of Africa and of black America, one can hardly fail to notice the wistful yearning for the 'health' and 'coherence' of African life that runs through many of his remarks on Africa. In the same essay in which he enumerated the cultural and psychological differences between the African and black American

116

situations, Baldwin sought also to explain what, in accordance with Senghor's views, he saw as the basic difference between the African and the Western concept of art. African art, he observed, was an instrument of social expression in a sense that Western art had never been. There was, in Africa, less of the insistence on the distinction between art and life that was so common in Western thought, and the concept of the artist's 'public' or 'audience' was one that was inimical to the African sense of the writer's relationship to his community. African art was pervasive, 'infinitely less special,' and was 'done by all, for all.' The mimetic principle in Western art was foreign to Africa, for here art was regarded as perishable, while what was lasting and perennial was 'the spirit which makes art possible.' [10] Baldwin was, of course, merely paraphrasing with approval the remarks made by Senghor at the Conference of Negro-African Writers and Artists held in Paris in 1956, and everyone knows by now how Senghor's Gallic intellectualisms often led him to a search for rigorous metaphysical categories that were just as foreign to the 'spirit' of African thought as the Western ideas which he himself sought to discredit. But what is of greater significance is the consideration that in summarising Senghor's opinions, Baldwin demonstrated a perhaps unconscious longing for the unified sensibility in African life which the accidents of history had precluded him from. It is, also, presumably in keeping with his belief that one cannot escape one's history that, despite his longing for a cultural life in which there was an integrated, healthy and coherent relationship between the writer and his environment, he should still voice an objection to this coherence that is nothing if not typically Western, namely, that

. . . a really cohesive society . . . has, generally . . . a much lower level of tolerance for the maverick, the dissenter, the man who steals the fire, than have societies in which, the common ground of belief having all but vanished, each man, in awful and brutal isolation, is for himself, to flower or to perish.[11]

Ultimately, then, it may be concluded that Baldwin's response to his African heritage is underscored both by an unwillingness to compromise the legitimacy and independence of black American culture and a wistful longing for that social coherence of which Senghor's Africa appeared to be so eminent an example. It seems, further, that in so far as he saw any advantages at all in being born in America, both the tone and the terminology of expression suggest that his was, in 1956, still a merely nascent political consciousness. He was in fact at the time just beginning his political education; the Algerian crisis was in its opening stages, and the Civil Rights Movement was still to come. Dien Bien Phu had already fallen, and Nkrumah's Ghana was soon to blaze the trail of African independence. All these events were destined to mould Baldwin's awareness of reality and to plunge him into the midst of political controversy, and his political attitudes in 1956 can hardly, therefore, be regarded as reliable indications of his mature consciousness.

A necessary corollary of Baldwin's ambiguous response to Africa is his equally ambiguous sense of his status in America. To unravel the precise details of this complementary vision is by no means an easy task, but it may be suggested that it derives fundamentally from a profound sense of paradox. Having, despite his longing, discounted the possibility of any real and useful links to Africa, he was obliged to discover some useful ground upon which he could base his claim to being American, and in the process he appears to have come to the paradoxical conclusion that to be black in America is to be at once an American Archetype and a sacrificial victim. The first was an argument from history, and the second derived from a mystical conception of the meaning of 'suffering'. From a historical perspective, it was not at all difficult for him to lay undisputed claim to citizenship in this country, and though Baldwin has himself never been particularly noted for any lyric celebration of this fact, his view of the matter, sardonically stated in *The Fire Next Time*—"I am not a ward of America; I am one of the first Americans to arrive on these shores"—is hardly different from Melvin Tolson's more elaborate claim in 'Dark Symphony'—

> My history-moulding ancestors
> Planted the first crop of wheat on these shores,

Built ships to conquer the Seven Seas
Erected the Cotton Empire,
Flung railroads across a hemisphere,
Disemboweled the earth's iron and coal,
Tunneled the mountains and bridged rivers,
Harvested the grain and hewed forests,
Sentineled the Thirteen Colonies,
Unfurled Old Glory at the North Pole,
Fought a hundred battles for the Republic.[12]

Undisputed though these contributions may be, there was, never-theless, an exquisite irony embedded in these recapitulations of history, since both Baldwin and Tolson appeared to base their claims on American citizenship upon qualifications that were not at all required of other Americans. A writer like Emerson or Whitman would clearly have found it preposterous to be obliged to justify his claims to America by having recourse to such qualifications of thankless travail; more pertinently, the European immigrants of more recent history could hardly begin to boast such sacrifices for America, even if they so wished, yet their claims to citizenship could be advanced with far greater plausibility than even Crispus Attucks could ever hope to achieve.

Baldwin, like many another black writer here, must clearly have been aware of this vexatious irony, first, because in so far as he had to justify his claims to citizenship by appealing to actual sacrifices, his was an almost unprecedented dilemma, and, secondly, because even an ungrudging admission by white Americans of these claims did not, ultimately, settle the issue. It is, in part, to this impregnable viciousness that Baldwin refers when he characterizes history as a nightmare. And operating from this presupposition of the night-marishness of history, the black American has generally sought to resolve his dilemma in two major ways. Either he truculently or defiantly asserted his American inheritance (both the Black Power militants and those who, from the argument of the 'territorial imperative,' demand that New Jersey become an exclusively black State appear as much to have embraced this alternative as the integrationists and assimilationists whom they villify) or, with Marcus

Garvey, he saw his condition here as a temporary quirk of history that must be resolved by his final return to Africa. Baldwin belongs, quite obviously, to the former category, but it is perhaps an indication of the essential agnosticism of his political imagination that his claims to America are ultimately not based, in fact, upon the argument from 'contributions', but rather upon a mystical conception of the moral significance of suffering. It would appear that for him the crucial question has never really been whether he is in fact an American, but whether, rather, he is justified in claiming an authority and moral superiority that few other Americans can lay claim to. The answer to this last question is, in the Baldwin corpus, a positive one, and it has quite often derived from his vision of the regenerative power of tribulation. It is doubtless easy to see in this view of suffering a romantic, sentimentalized effort at psychic compensation, an implausible attempt to make the best of an intolerably tragic condition. But if we bore in mind the potency of mythological beliefs in white American culture, the role, for instance, that the myth of inherent white supremacy (or the Southern lady as aesthetic paragon) has played in American history, it would become clear that in the realm of socio-political behaviour, mythic faith can be an intensely palpable and utilitarian justification for all sorts of action. In any case, it seems reasonable to suggest that Baldwin's prophetic stance, the moral outrage of his essays, the eloquent authority with which he has often called upon both whites and blacks to rise above themselves, would all seem painfully comic were we to fail to understand the presuppositions upon which they are founded.

Baldwin's most sustained presentation of this view of suffering appears in *The Fire Next Time*. In this essay he came to the daring conclusion that black history in America has been 'something very beautiful', and to underline this paradoxical faith, he prefaced his conclusion with a description of this history that is decidedly horrifying:

This past, the Negro's past, of rope, fire, torture, castration, infanticide, rape; death and humiliation; fear by day and night, fear as deep as the marrow of the bone; doubt that he was worthy of life, since every one around him denied it; sorrow for his women, for his kinfolk, for his children, who needed his protection, and whom he could not protect; rage, hatred, and murder, hatred for white men so deep that it often turned against him and his own, and made all love, all trust, all joy impossible— this past, this endless struggle to achieve and reveal and confirm a human identity, human authority, yet contains, for all its horror, something very beautiful.[13]

The beauty of this nightmare derives, not from the denial of pain, but precisely, from the black man's ability to turn his political dispossession to moral advantage. He is a morally superior being because he has suffered, for "people who cannot suffer, can never grow up, can never discover who they are."

That man who is forced each day to snatch his manhood, his identity out of the fire of human cruelty that rages to destroy it knows, if he survives his effort. . . . something about himself and human life that no school on earth—and, indeed, no church— can teach.[14]

It is this secret knowledge, strained from an interminably painful experience, that defines the black man; it is this, too, that makes him ideal as an instrument of moral regeneration in American life. According to Baldwin, then, an adequately meaningful view of black history must encompass both the agony and the ecstasy of blackness. The supreme advantage of this interpretation of black history lies precisely in its ability to accommodate and explain both past and present travail. Indeed, its particular attraction appears to lie on the consideration that the magnitude of the consolation it offers is in exact proportion to the enormity of the pain and tragedy it describes. Thus, an essential organising principle behind Baldwin's social essays—'The Harlem Ghetto,' 'Notes of a Native Son,' 'Fifth Avenue, Uptown,' 'East River, Downtown,' and 'Nobody knows my Name'—is in fact a less than obvious one. They represent not so much a sense of outrage or an impassioned call for change, as they underscore an abiding faith that the black man is destined, at some indeterminate point in the future, to be the salvation of this land, a task for which he is preeminently qualified by virtue of his prolonged stewardship in suffering.

Despite the conceptual neatness of the view of Baldwin's response to blackness here presented, it seems necessary to observe, also, that the moral conclusions that he derived, in *The Fire Next Time*, from the evidence of political oppression were, at best, inconclusive, and at worst, the result of a 'confusion of realms.'[15] The blithely nonchalant manner in which he characteristically regarded the socio-political and the ethico-moral realms as interchangeable was one that a Machiavelli would clearly have found quite outrageous, and to this extent he could, we suppose, properly be charged with having contributed to whatever confusions there are today in black thought. As we have already suggested, the essential thrust of his observations on, and interpretations of, history was a moral one; his theory of suffering, like his definition of freedom and love, was fundamentally 'moral', in so far as it derived not from an economic or political view of racism but from what appears to be a neo-Platonic concern with goodness and virtue. Often implicit in his attitude was the temptation to suppose that virtue was a necessary and sufficient condition for good citizenship; and profound and moving as his portraits of the black man's travails often were, his conclusions were at the same time, therefore, often limited by a rather ancient definition of 'society'. In his earlier essays, in particular, the persona of the sermonizing pastor tended often to engulf the voice of the political critic, and rarely, until quite recently, did he demonstrate any unambiguous awareness of the power and influence of impersonal forces over the lives of individuals. Consequently, one often left with a feeling of indigestion after reading his essays: the description was clear and forceful, but the resolutions offered were largely unusable except as doses for psychic sustenance. Baldwin must himself no doubt have been aware of this limitation, for his most recent essay, *No Name in the Street*, indicates a clear movement away from the postulation of moral precepts to the presentation of more concretely political choices.

To the extent that the predominant element of his vision of blackness is the assumption of a moral superiority that is the outcome of centuries of unrelieved suffering and is offered as the most probable source of regeneration in America, it would appear that this particular resolution of the agony is an unusual one—one that though implicit even in Garvey's thoughts was yet unemphasized in black thought until quite recently. That this has been a significant cause of the uneasy response of many black critics to Baldwin is perhaps an indication both of the peculiarity of the latter's views and of the difficulty involved in any attempt to draw meaningful conclusions from contemporary history. From the virtuously indignant lady who once accused Baldwin of being 'an extremely talented literary prostitute,'[16] to Julian Mayfield who expressed the more sombre wish that Baldwin, distinguished writer though he is, were more of a scholar;[17] from Eldridge Cleaver, whose criticism is more polemical than judicious,[18] to Harold Cruse, who in his magisterial and all-embracing contempt dismisses Baldwin as lacking totally in historical perspective and as being ignorant of the realities of black life,[19] the burden of the charge against Baldwin has often been that in his insistence on a moral interpretation of life, he has tended to overlook the more salient and realistic implications of the black American's social and political oppression. What is, however, not too often recognised is that in spite of its more positively political orientation, there is implicit in the thought of such other writers as LeRoi Jones (Imamu Baraka), Larry Neal, Ron Karenga and Don Lee an assumption of the moral preeminence of blackness that could quite legitimately be seen as deriving, in part at least, from Baldwin. The contemporary concept of the beauty of blackness can hardly otherwise be considered meaningful were we not to assume for it a necessary ethical ambience. And if this is true, it should be clear that the consciousness of these younger writers, despite their significant theoretical departures, belongs indeed to a continuing black tradition in thought.

To identify the links in this tradition is not, however, to underestimate the outstanding contributions of such radical writers and thinkers as Baraka and Karenga. The crucial and historic achievement of these men and women has been the manner in which they have sought to provide a usable and unified theory of blackness in which there is little distinction between thought, art and life. We have seen how, in one of his earlier essays, Baldwin attempted to summarize with approval Senghor's view of the unity of art and life in traditional African culture. It was, however, to be the singular contribution of Ron Karenga to employ the African paradigm in the development of his concept of the Black Aesthetic.[20] As we shall see, the adoption of the African paradigm did not by any means imply that African realities were entirely identical to black American ones, but it must be emphasized that Karenga's theory of the Black Aesthetic, though by no means definitive, was quite successful in 'solving' two fundamental problems. The first had to do with the supposed incompatibility between ideology and significant art, the second, with the perennial issue of the responsibilities of the artist to his community.

With regard to the first problem, the application of the African example made it possible for the writer theoretically, at least, to take his calling seriously without at the same time being unduly concerned with perpetuating his memory. Horace's *exegi monumentum* was, in other words, a peculiarly 'Western' attitude that in part implied that the writer had a personal stake in the quality of his works that went far beyond his responsibility to reflect and record the spirit of his community. A basic presupposition of the African concept, according to Senghor at any rate, was that the artefact was in fact meant to be perishable, to be less lasting than brass, to be eroded by rain and biting wind.[21] The monument that the African artist sought to erect was not to his name, but to the spirit that engendered his work. Clearly a theory of art to which Eliot's distinctions between tradition and the individual talent were largely inapplicable, in which there was no conscious desire on the writer's part to perpetuate his own memory rendered it irrelevant to dwell upon such issues as the proper employment of ideology and didacticism in art, since art belonged to the community and was a direct expression of the community's aspirations and attitudes. Further, this communal concept of art immediately transformed the thorny issue of 'beauty' in art, since it became no longer simply a matter of aesthetics, but one in which utilitarian values were openly and unashamedly involved.

On the question of the responsibilities of the artist, Karenga's in-

sistence that Black art must be 'functional, collective and committing' was a positive choice in favour of the social, communal implications of art.[22] Art was the property of the community; it derived
not so much from genius or inspiration as from the artist's participation in a communal spirit; there was no 'audience' distinct and
separate from the artist, and his obligation was therefore not so
much to testify to an individual vision as to articulate the feelings
of the group. The artist was, then, in a quite fundamental sense a
mouthpiece, an instrument by which his community expressed itself; his failure was a communal failure, his success a credit to the
group. We shall in a moment attempt to identify one of the unfortunate consequences of this theory of art, but it must also be observed that though Karenga's view leaves certain questions of detail unanswered, it does in fact manage more successfully to avoid
that obsessive egocentricity that has plagued Western attitudes to
art from Homer to Horace, and from Keats to Hemingway.

There was nothing particularly inevitable in this development,
but there is hardly any doubt now that Karenga's theory has sometimes led to an unduly constricted vision of Blackness, to an unwise
reluctance to admit fully the continuities in the black tradition in
thought and art. A good many of those who have adopted this
theory have, mistakenly in our opinion, tended to assume that the
concept of the Black Aesthetic is applicable only to works produced during the last decade. But nothing could be farther from
the truth of the matter, for, as we have tried to argue, in so far as we
can see the effort and achievement of most black writers in this
country as being underscored and indeed motivated by a painful
agony that needed to be resolved, the particular resolutions which
individual writers have presented, antagonistic as they often are,
must nevertheless be seen as being no more significant than the
identical intention that motivated them. In more precise terms, to
seek to expel (as some black critics have sought to do) such writers
as Baldwin, Ellison and Wright from the tradition encompassed by
the Black Aesthetic on grounds of ideological inadequacy is, ironically, to deny that a long-standing tradition does in fact exist.
There is hardly any need to go into all the issues raised by this concept, but part of the problem clearly derives from our attempts to

125

impose rigorous exactitudes upon a subject (namely, 'blackness') that is almost by definition incapable of sustaining them. There is, in our condition, an understandable yearning for clarifications, for conceptual order, for a neatly structured vision of life, and in this context the search for orders and hierarchies of blackness is a perfectly legitimate one. It is legitimate to ask the question whether or not Malcolm X belonged to a higher realm of consciousness than did Booker T. Washington; but to deduce from this question the assumption that these two thinkers did not therefore belong to the same tradition is to lack that subtlety of historical vision which is presumed to be one significant advantage that hindsight bestows. Discriminations and comparisons are useful and necessary, but they cannot properly be employed as the justification for expelling large numbers of black writers from the pantheon of Black art and thought.

Perhaps one useful way of clarifying the issue being raised here is by having recourse to the Platonic notion of the Idea of a thing and its actual, phenomenal representation. Assume, for a moment, that the Idea of Blackness, like the Christian Idea of Virtue, is an inexhaustible one. It becomes immediately possible to conceive of a situation in which Phylis Wheatley, Paul Dunbar, Marcus Garvey, Booker T. Washington, James Baldwin, Malcolm X and Angela Davis (to name a few random examples) are particular manifestations of an identical aspiration toward the ultimate Idea of Blackness. In such a situation discriminations are obviously possible, and certainly necessary; one can, and should evaluate the relative levels of blackness which Washington and Garvey attained. It is equally clear that even if we decided that Garvey was 'blacker' than Washington, such a discrimination cannot properly be employed as a means of expelling the latter from participation in the all-encompassing Idea or Fountain of Blackness. The argument above does not pretend to resolve all the problems raised by the issue of blackness[23] but, like the African paradigm referred to earlier, the 'neo-Platonic' concept of Blackness has the advantage of emphasizing the contributions of the community over those of the individual and of reestablishing the participation of all black men and women in the agony and the ecstasy of blackness which, presumably, is the ultimate intent that justifies the evolution of the concept of the Black Aesthetic.

Eminently useful though the incorporation of the African view of art into the concept of the Black Aesthetic is, it is important to emphasize that the adoption of the African paradigm does not by any means suggest that the realities that engendered it are identical to those that led to the evolution of the concept of the Black Aesthetic in America. 'Linkages' there certainly are between the fatherland and the black communities of the diaspora, and there is little reason to suppose that the theory of the Black Aesthetic cannot function as effectively in contemporary Africa (which is certainly in dire need of some useful principles) as it does here, but in view of the general tendency to assume that the black creative sensibility in America has been little affected by the accidents of history,[24] it is necessary to examine here in some detail an important area in which the sensibility of a man like Baldwin significantly differs from that of say, Chinua Achebe, and thereby suggest that Baldwin may not be entirely wrong in his basic conclusion that his responses are often different from those of his contemporaries in Africa.

III

When, in *The Presidential Papers*, Norman Mailer put forward the not-so-original thesis that there is a direct connection between the heightened sexuality of the lower classes and their condition of oppression, no one was willing to accuse him, despite the numerous roles he has assumed over the years, of having attempted to set himself up as a spokesman for the black American.[25] It did not really matter that his major preoccupations were hardly 'racial,' nor that he had been primarily concerned with the sexual confusions of America's white middle class. What was more significant was that years later Eldridge Cleaver, who may be supposed once to have been a more authentic spokesman for the dispossessed, was sufficiently impressed by Mailer's argument to juxtapose him, in his search for corroboration from the 'masters,' with Karl Marx. It is possible to suggest that Cleaver's essay, 'the Primeval Mitosis'[26] is a rather unsuccessful attempt to provide a quasi-scientific explanation for what properly belongs in the realm of psycho-mythology—and we are referring specifically to the distinctions he draws between the 'White Omnipotent Administrator' and the 'Black Supermasculine Menial.' It could also be argued that in seeking to articulate and to develop into a system a number of attitudes and assumptions that are still undeniable elements of popular mores in this country, Cleaver did make a useful contribution toward the resolution of racial controversies here. Part of the importance of this essay lay, of course, in the sheer boldness of Cleaver's attempt, in the exhilarating manner in which he sought to surpass Marx by extending the latter's class theories into racial ones; but what is to us of particular significance is that he could not, it appears, find any positive role in his intellectual construct for the black woman, thereby dramatizing one of the crucial peculiarities of racial attitudes here, namely, the near-tragic predicament of the black female in America. In assuring us that the white female was the authentic, 'psychic bride' of the black male, he basically restated what is no less than an essential element of the popular imagination here, but what was more interesting was the implication, consequent upon this assurance, that the black female is only technically, in an immediate and less than profound sense, the black man's bride. It was not that he rejoiced in this state of affairs, as he clearly demonstrates in another essay, 'To All Black Women, From All Black Men,' but when he argues that the details and degree of black sexuality are a consequence of oppression and at the same time suggests that this sexuality is primarily directed outward, toward the white male and female, it becomes clear that the issue is by no means a simple one, and that it deserves more than the kind of attention that sociologists have given the matter. For if it is true that heightened sexuality is a consequence of oppression, one might reasonably expect that the very condition of oppression would make it near-impossible for the black male to mate with the white woman. Reality, however, belies this expectation, and sociological explanation merely compounds the contradictions involved. At the point where sociology collapses, theories of psychological determinism take over, but even with the theories of guilt and rebellious iconoclasm, of fantasy and psychic compensations, it is hardly necessary to observe that the matter is by no means sufficiently clarified or explained away.

Whatever the truth of the matter may be, it can be firmly stated that the fact of sexual conflict, of incompatibility between the black man and woman is a presupposition cardinal to Cleaver's thesis in 'The Primeval Mitosis.' Now, with respect to attitudes in the black community, Cleaver's may be a reliable vision, but it is quite clearly not a unanimous one. Where he presupposes a state of conflict in sexual relations within the black community, there is, too, the view that insists not only on the sexual heroism of the black male, but also, and perhaps with even greater intensity, on the incomparable unity and perfection of intramural sexual relations in the black community. We have in mind here the kind of view championed by *Essence Magazine*, the view that the black male is a superstud whose heroic powers are most dramatically realised in his relations with the black woman. There is to our mind something unduly limiting and embarassing in this definition of the contemporary black man as Homo Sexualis, but it would be foolish to ignore an attitude that has so powerfully taken hold of the imagination of Americans, from Norman Mailer and Jack Kerouac to the gentlemen who produced the movies *Sweet Sweetback* and *Shaft.*

We may identify, then, two antagonistic views of sexuality in the popular imagination of the black community—the view of sexual conflict in which the black male's sexual drives are directed outward, toward the white female; and the view of intramural sexual utopia, in which the black male and female are inseparable partners in a sexual Eden. But the major concern here is not with the realities of the popular imagination, intriguing as these are, but with the uses of the rhetoric of sexuality in black fiction in America. What we call the popular imagination is the sum total of intuitions, persuasions, of shades and intensitites of prejudice and opinion, each of which can, if abstracted from the whole, stand more or less on its own. And because of this potential for individual existence which its various components have, the popular imagination is often quite impossible of analysis, except in so far as we can provide a description of it. In this regard then—the intramural and the outward—directed views of sexuality in the black community are, though essentially complementary, each capable of standing alone. But our ideal conception of a work of art rests essentially on the indivisibility of its components, on the integrity of vision that informs it. The fundamental distinction to be drawn, therefore, between the popular and the creative imagination is precisely this, that where, in the popular imagination, the intramural view almost automatically demands a dialectical consciousness of a 'contradictory complement,' there appears, for the creative imagination, to be hardly any need for preclusions, even in a dialectical sense, since sexuality is here often not conceived as an engagement involving two persons, but primarily as a unilateral assertion of the sexual hero's justification for being. Thus, in Richard Wright's *Native Son*, Bigger's responses to his black girl-friend Bessie are basically indistinguishable from his reactions to the white girl Mary Dalton, except in so far as his desires toward the latter are unconsummated. Consider, for example, the tone of Wright's account of Bigger's intercourse with Bessie:

> Her voice came to him from a deep, far-away silence and he paid her no heed. The loud demand of the tensity of his own body was a voice that drowned out hers . . . He was conscious of nothing but her and what he wanted. He flung the cover back, ignoring the cold, and not knowing that he did it. Bessie's hands were on his chest, her fingers spreading protestingly open, pushing him away. He heard her give a soft moan that seemed not to end . . . Imperiously driven, he rode rough-shod over her whimpering protests, feeling acutely sorry for her as he gallopped a frenzied horse down a steep hill in the face of a resisting wind.[27]

We must bear in mind that Bigger is, in his own way, 'in love' with Bessie, to the extent, that is, that he is capable of loving anyone. Yet we have here a powerful impression of coercion and resistance, of a struggle almost unto the death. It seems clear that in this episode sexuality is conceived of primarily as a unilateral act of self-assertion, a condition in which Bessie's existence is merely an extension, as it were, of Bigger's embattled heroism. Now, Bessie is black, and Wright quite clearly does not, certainly not in *Native Son*, believe in the notion of intramural sexual bliss in the black community. Some would probably object that Wright's attitude here is far from representative of contemporary sensibilities, that his 'hatred' of his own kind is a function of his 'Negroness' (as distinct from his blackness): a self-hatred that has long since been superceded by a more healthy attitude to self. But it would appear that such objections are useful only in as much as they imply a desire for a more ideal situation, since any close examination of more recent fiction will indicate that the situation remains essentially unchanged. It seems futile to argue that Bigger's unilateral and bellicose sexuality is an indication either of his sense of inferiority or of his hatred for black women, for, as we have suggested, there is little reason to believe that Mary Dalton would have fared better with him, despite the fact that she is described as being as close to Cleaver's definition of the 'ultrafeminine' (her communist connections notwithstanding) white woman as we can find anywhere.

If Richard Wright in *Native Son* represents that fictional sensibility in which the black hero's unilateral sexuality is directed primarily against black women, James Baldwin provides for us the essential complement to this vision; for the sexuality of his black heroes is often directed, not against the black Amazon, but against the white, ultrafeminine female. More than twenty years after the publication of *Native Son*, Baldwin was to present to us a vision of black sexual heroism that was just as fundamentally egocentric as Wright's, except that in Baldwin's novels the absoluteness of the unilateral principle becomes much more apparent. In his fiction, the black sexual hero is a lonely figure, a black and awesome satyr isolated from everyone else precisely at the moment when he seeks, through his sexual powers, to assert his humanity. In *Go Tell It on the Mountain*, Gabriel's relations with women are characterised most essentially by an egocentric drive to obliterate that cooperative engagement that can transform the sexual act from passion into love. Neither in his affair with Esther or the strangely erotic woman from out of town, nor in his marital life with Deborah and Elizabeth does he regard his partners as anything more than neutral mediums through whom his heroism is demonstrated and jus-

131

tified. Indeed, quite often, as in his life with his first wife Deborah, it is as though he feels that his women are eternally obligated to him for being the chosen vessels through which his heroism must flower.

But nothing more dramatically illustrates the curious continuities of this egocentric sensibility than Baldwin's third novel, *Another Country*. This novel is, in respect of the sexual relations between its characters, a much more complicated novel than any of Wright's fictions. For one thing, it re-enacts and extends the outward-directed principle in the black sexual imagination: quite apart from Rufus' relations with Leona, Ida, the vengeful black nemesis of this novel, not only goes out into the white community in search of sexual relations, but also these affairs are in themselves also construed as weapons of racial retribution. In all her terrible and single-minded grandeur, she is the ultimate black sexual heroine, aware of her beauty and the bounties she can confer, but her men have to pay a near-insupportable price for the privilege she grants; they must know no peace of mind, ridden as they are with guilt and remorse. Secondly, *Another Country* is one of the few black novels in which the egocentric principle is pushed to its outermost limits. There is in this novel the intimation, at least, that homosexual relations may in fact be seen as an attempt to symbolically renounce the significance of engagement in sex, whether of the outward-directed or the intramural kind. For if we see homosexuality as springing partly from a narcissistic desire to return to the self in search of sexual fulfilment, unencumbered by the procreative potential of it all, it becomes clear that what we then have is but a blatant affirmation of the egocentric sexual principle. But nothing is more intriguing than the strange similarities between descriptions of intercourse in both Wright and Baldwin, and this in spite of the many fundamental differences in the attitudes to life of these two writers. We have seen how, in the love-making episode cited above, the operative image is that of conflict, of antagonism. The passage is replete with such terms as 'drive,' 'ride roughshod,' 'gallop,' 'frenzy.' Consider in this light, then, the following passage from *Another Country*, in which Rufus is making love to Leona:

Then, from the center of his rising storm, very slowly and deliberately, he began the slow ride home. And she carried him, as the sea will carry a boat . . . They murmured and sobbed on this journey, he softly, insistently cursed. Each labored to reach a harbour; there could be no rest until this motion became unbearably accelerated by the power that was rising in them both. Rufus opened his eyes for a moment and watched her face, which was transfigured with agony . . . and in spite of himself he began moving faster, thrusting deeper. He wanted her to remember him the longest day she lived . . . Under his breath he cursed the milk-white bitch and groaned and rode his weapon between her thighs. She began to cry . . . and at once he felt himself strangling, about to explode or die. A moan and a curse tore through him while he beat her with all the strength he had.[28]

The similarities between these two passages, both in imagery and in conception, speak for themselves. And in view of this identity of sexual vision between two such major writers, it seems necessary to examine the implications of this state of affairs.

It would appear that in the imagination of these writers, the fundamental characteristic of sexual relations is that of conflict—a conflict in which the belligerents strive to defend their individuality. It would further appear that in such a conflict the male partner is obligated to be the victor, and through his triumph he at once achieves a negation of the female partner's validity as a being and an assertion of his own heroic, if isolated existence. But the sensibility here identified in Baldwin and Wright is not, strictly speaking, a 'pornographic' one, for the crucial difference between the sexuality of black fiction and the pornographic imagination is that while, in the latter, the participants are *both* interchangeable and therefore mere sexual objects, the situation in black fiction is not a reversible one. That is to say, that very seldom in black fiction in this country (John A. Williams' *Sissie* is one exception that comes immediately to mind) do we see the female partner assuming the role of the male and vice versa. Even in terms of physical postures, the female is most often the vessel that is 'driven' or 'ridden,' and the male is the one who does the driving.

Despite, however, this fundamental distinction between the sexual sensibility of a Baldwin and the pornographic imagination, there is another perspective from which the belligerent, egocentric sexuality of black fiction may be seen to run dangerously close to pornography;[29] true enough, the 'erotic imperative' is but one of the countless imperatives in contemporary art, and black fiction does appear to have its other imperatives too. It would be false to maintain that in black fiction all action is reducible to the demands of the erotic imperative, but there does seem to be sufficient ground to suggest that our novelists sometimes tend to confuse mere eroticism with 'love.' We are told that Rufus 'loves' Leona in *Another Country*, that Gabriel loves Deborah in *Go Tell It on the Mountain*, and that Bigger loves Bessie in *Native Son*. Yet as we observe the manifestations of this love, we find little more than the enthusiastic interest in mechanical expertise. Quite often the ability to induce or inspire orgasmic titillation appears to be construed not simply as an erotic end in itself but as the outward manifestation of an inner, more profound feeling which we hardly ever see actualized. Again, as we observe the undisputed sexual preeminence of the black hero, we often are led to ask whether we are being offered a new vision of universal man (black) in which sexual expertise is thought to be a useful symbol of his vitality as a human being. And if we have thus come to a point in black culture at which sexual prowess has taken over such other traditional symbols as courage in war and wisdom in juridical deliberations, it would be fair to suggest then that the limitations of such a perspective on life are only too disturbingly clear. Baldwin's record, in this regard, is in fact a good deal more complex than the conclusions reached here might suggest. For one thing, his women appear to be more capable of giving love, and it is partly because his black women are so often 'brutalized' by their men that they become the authentic repositories of a vital, regenerative force that could presumably transform their world; and for another thing, he has begun, in his most recent writing, to reach a conceptual position in which homosexuality is no longer simply a means of self-assertion but of communal growth. (See our discussion of *Tell Me How Long the Train's Been Gone* in Chapter Seven).

In making these observations, it is not our intention to imply that our novelists are incapable of drawing the proper distinction between mere eroticism and love, but we do contend that even when they demonstrate a *theoretical* awareness of this distinction, the *actual* rhetoric employed tends to suggest that true love is impossible of realisation, and must be left on the level of wistful aspiration, of unattainable ideal. That is to say that both in terms of concrete description and of dramatic plausibility the physical sexuality of the black hero is often more convincing than his ability to or even capacity for, love. Quite often, indeed, there is a measure of auctorial intervention in the plot, consciously, it seems, calculated to ensure the death of love—an intervention, we may add, that is not essential to the development of the dramatic situation. Two interesting examples would be the collapse, or at least the stagnation of the love relationship between Iris and Time in Williams' *Sissie*, and the death of Richard, Elizabeth's first love and John's father in Baldwin's *Go Tell*. But it would perhaps be more rewarding to consider for a moment what happens to Max and Lilian in Williams' *The Man Who Cried I Am*. Max Reddick is black, educated, embattled, and in search of a job. He meets and, we are told, falls in love with Lilian, a young, beautiful and black High School teacher; he would marry her, but she prefers to wait until he has a stable job and can provide for her all the things that suburban American wives dream of. In the mean time she becomes pregnant and would rather have an abortion than be married to an unemployed man. And so she dies of a post-operative haemorrhage. Now, there are in this episode compelling external reasons why Lilian dies and Max is left bereft, and the author wastes no time in assuring us that racism is at the root of the matter. But quite apart from these external reasons, what impresses us most is not the plausibility of Williams' realism here, but the nagging suspicion we have that such a relationship was doomed in any case to collapse, precisely because neither Max nor Lilian is capable of any measure of self-denial or sacrifice. The situation becomes even more disturbing when we see Max subsequently take to wife a Dutch woman, and when we further observe that the basic quality of their married life is an unending and rather tedious luxuriation in sexuality. It is quite in the nature of the thing itself that the marriage does not last beyond the point of erotic satiation, beyond the point, that is, where marriage is conceived of primarily as an arena for the realisation of sexual possibilities.

The situation can be seen, then, on two levels. On the most negative level, the writers here mentioned (and many more: Bullins in 'Going A'Buffalo,' LeRoi Jones in 'Experimental Death Unit No. I') appear to be at least more inclined to discourage any interpretation of love that encompasses more than the erotic relationship itself, and on the more positive side they appear to conceive of sexuality in terms of a conflict situation—one which is then reduced to the level of the male egocentric principle in which the female becomes merely a dispensable medium for the validation of a curious form of heroism. Here, then, is the crux of the matter. We are confronted with a strange situation in which the popular imagination appears to be more complex than the creative vision. The former, despite its contradictions does, at least in part, concede that both sexual bliss and 'love' are quite realisable within the black community, whereas the creative vision seems to deal in stiff and exclusive absolutes. And if all this is true we may then, in passing, ask whether the alleged inviolability of the creative vision is not an ambiguous, double-edged notion, one that both allows the potential for articulation and prophecy, and at the same time becomes the medium of the writer's alienation from the cultural sources of his existence. The responsible critic is in such a situation obliged to suggest the probability that there does exist a condition in which there appears to be a clear and growing dichotomy between a fundamental creed of the contemporary black psyche—that black is beautiful—and what seems to us to be a persistent creative modification of that creed: the black male is a rare sexual bird, and the black female is an adorable but still disposable plastic drinking cup. (As a means of resolving this dichotomy, Karenga's prescriptions are, clearly, eminently applicable here, since he does at least seek to ensure that the writer's sensibility is regulated, for better or for worse, by the dialectics of the popular imagination.) And since it is part of the ultimate intention here to provide some further perspective on Baldwin's achievements and limitations, it is well worth mentioning (an issue which we discuss in a little more detail in a later chapter) that Baldwin appears to have discovered a conceptual solution to this problem, in so far as he sees sexuality, if only in the homosexual sense, as a potential for regeneration, *within the black community*.

The situation in African literature is a rather different one. To anyone familiar with Frobenius' *African Nights* or Yambo Ouloguem's recent novel, *Bound to Violence*, it might appear that there are hardly any serious differences to be observed, in respect of the treatment of love and sexuality, between African and black American fiction; but such a conclusion would be most misleading indeed. Frobenius' tales belong essentially to the popular tradition, and the apparently limitless freedom of imagination of these stories is one that we hardly find in more consciously literary productions. (Ouloguem's novel is, on the other hand, an accomplished novel, but as we shall see in a moment, its intentions are in fact far from 'sexual'.) Consequently, a useful preliminary observation would be that where the sexual imagination of black fiction in this country tends to be clamorous and assertive, African fiction, in terms of its concern with love and sexuality, appears to have as its characteristic dynamic the rhetoric of reticence.

Chinua Achebe's novels provide a useful illustration of this observation. Love and sexuality are hardly major concerns in *Things Fall Apart*, but a consideration of the love relationship between Okonkwo, the hero of the novel, and his wife Ekwefi would be worth our while. It may safely be stated that theirs is a union of love, since she feels constrained to leave her first husband to run to Okonkwo, thus fulfilling a long-standing dream. But neither in respect of their feelings for each other nor in the manifestation of these feelings are we offered anything like an exhaustive description of the situation:

She had married Anene because Okonkwo was too poor then to marry. Two years after her marriage to Anene she could bear it no longer and she ran away to Okonkwo. It had been early in the morning. The moon was shining. She was going to the stream to fetch water. Okonkwo's house was on the way to the stream. She went in and knocked on his door and he came out. Even in those

137

days he was not a man of many words. He just carried her into his bed and in the darkness began to feel around her waist for the loose end of her cloth.[30]

Here we have in a nutshell the type of 'reticence' we referred to above. An analysis of this passage will indicate that there are a large number of assumptions implied here which Achebe expects his readers to recognise. Okonkwo may not be a man of many words, but his actions are understood to be eloquent enough, for by the one single act of taking Ekwefi into his bed the ostensibly adulterous episode is transformed into a passionate consummation of wedlock. Sexuality is conceived of here not merely as an erotic end in itself, but as part of an integrated response to life in which love is not just an unattainable ideal but a perfectly realisable objective. This is the closest we come to finding an erotic description of sex in *Things Fall Apart*, and since this is by far the best novel Achebe has so far written, it is tempting to surmise that he has some inner design in mind. There are, to be sure, token notices of sexuality in his later novels, but in terms of its dramatic function in these novels, it may be argued that Achebe often employs his cryptic descriptions of sexuality to denote moral differentiations in his characters. In *No Longer At Ease*, for instance, the somewhat depersonalised sexual relationships are conceived of primarily as indicators of the growing disintegration of traditional moral values. When Obi Okonkwo sleeps with the nameless girl who offers her body to obtain a scholarship, we are asked to understand that he does this precisely because he has come to feel that morality has no longer any categorical sanctions—a conviction that leads, in turn, to his own moral collapse. Equally, in *A Man of the People*, Chief Nanga's promiscuous relationships are indices of his moral turpitude. There is, in sum, no celebration of sexuality in Achebe's novels. To the extent that he deals with the issue at all, it is often as though he is using the condition to make moral comments on his characters (an interesting situation since it would then follow that the elder Okonkwo in *Things Fall* is morally superior to his grandson in *No Longer at Ease* and to Chief Nanga in *A Man of the People*).

But the rhetoric of reticence, as it appears in Achebe's novels, is not the only version of sexuality that we have in African fiction. He employs his descriptions of sexuality as a means of moral discriminations, it is true, but if we approached his dramatic situations from a psychological perspective, we would probably have to conclude that the link he seeks to establish between sexuality and ethics is an unduly arbitrary one, and that the very attempt in itself indicates a certain level of psychic unease or repression, since it appears to be so much out of tune with the exuberance of the oral tradition in Africa. However, if Achebe's differentiations are a little forced, Mongo Beti is perhaps more successful in identifying the moral perspective of sexuality without converting it into a rigid principle of moral differentiation. In *Mission to Kala*, for instance, there is a much more hilarious engagement in sexuality. Most of the people in the little village of Kala, and especially the heretical gang of young rogues, appear to engage in, or at least to be undisturbed by promiscuity. There is a kind of libertinism in this novel that, if considered out of context, could lead to a serious misconception of Beti's intentions here. The young men of the village may indulge their sexual fantasies and their esoteric categories of virility, but they are also aware that their exuberance can in no sense be seen as an alternative to, or a meaningful act of rebellion against traditional ethics. The very motive for young Medza's appearance in Kala illustrates this point. The young woman who runs away from her less than sympathetic husband knows that she may opt to move in with another man, but it is also made perfectly clear that she may do this only at the risk of the serious consequences that attend this option, and it is worth observing that though she does suffer from public blame when the matter is adjudicated, it is her adulterous mate who is made to pay the full price for his complicity in midsdemeanour. Sexuality is in this novel, then, not an abnormality (nor does Beti seek to set it up as a rigid standard for moral judgment) but he does make it clear, we believe, that frivolity can only be tolerated so long as it does not radically threaten the health of the social weal.

Achebe and Beti are, as all artists have in some measure to be, 'moralists,' but where Achebe establishes an artificial link between sexuality and ethics, and thereby creates a conflict that does not really exist in practice, Beti manages to synthesize more successfully what are but two complementary aspects of the culture—an unromanticised sexual exuberance and the necessity to contain this within a broader ethical framework. By the same token, and despite the superficial similarities between Ouloguem's sensibility in *Bound to Violence* and certain trends in black American fiction, the vision of sexuality in this novel is an essentially African one. The novel is an intensely erotic one, often pornographic in the fullest sense of that term, and even more often one gets the impression that it is a study in sexual violence. In many respects it reads like an over-intellectualized European novel, but where sexual heroism is in black American fiction at once a symbol of liberation and of alienation, Ouloguem's rendering of sexuality suggests that he conceives of it not as ecstatic celebration but as an index of moral degeneracy. The men and women who indulge in these countless sexual orgies are victims, not heroes; we certainly do not see them as Promethean heralds of a new age or of a new religion. Their frenetic concupiscence is presented as a mirror, as it were, through which one can look into the extent to which the spiritual foundations of their culture have become atrophied. Ultimately, then, Ouloguem is just as much a sexual moralist as Beti and Achebe are. Achebe achieves his intention through reticence, Beti through satire and caricature, and Ouloguem through the sheer volume of often nauseating promiscuity; and between them we thus have a representative African perspective on sexuality. Whatever the literary techniques they employ, they all three appear to agree on the fundamental issue that sexual potency can neither usefully be seen as an adequate substitute for more traditional forms of heroism nor as a symbol of individual liberation.

With respect to the supposed links between African and black American literature the conclusions to be drawn from the above analysis suggest that Baldwin's may well be a perfectly healthy, if unpopular scepticism, for whatever such links may be, they appear to be more recognisable in the more oral forms of literature (in the similarities, for instance, in the popular sexual imaginations of the two continents) and certainly do not encompass the question of the function of sexuality in fiction. Where it is presented often in black

American fiction as a positive index of heroic liberation, it is construed in African fiction at worst as something to be ashamed of, an index of moral degeneracy, and at best as an aspect of the culture that may be tolerated so long as it can be accommodated without any radical upheavals in the culture. It may be objected that the distinctions we have here established are unduly arbitrary, both because the examples chosen are not sufficiently representative, and because sexual attitudes and practices in black America are direct outgrowths of a racist culture. On the first charge, it does not appear to us likely that a more exhaustive illustration of our thesis would either enhance or detract from its plausibility, and all selective illustrations are in any case arbitrary. The second objection is a much more fundamental one, and we shall dare here to offer some opinion on the matter. Calvin Hernton's book, *Sex and Racism in America* is one of the most significant contributions to the thesis that sexuality in black America is inseparable from, and indeed the direct consequence of racial attitudes in the United States, and his arguments are often irrefutable. But if we insist, as we must, that the sensibility of the black American has undergone dramatic changes in recent years, if we insist that there has been in this period a momentous rediscovery of innate nobility, of pride in black culture and of the black man's capacity to initiate and modify myths, it follows that the argument from racism, which may have been perfectly plausible at the time Mr. Hernton wrote his book, would have to be modified to accommodate ideas and motivations that now *originate* from the black community itself. There can be no doubt that as recently as two decades ago, the black man's psychological responses were more severely limited and predetermined by external social factors over which he had little control, and he may at the time quite legitimately have sought to compensate for his social dispossession by laying claim to a sexual heroism that was psychically functional but hardly adequate as a response to his more than palpable socio-economic pain—and the myth-makers of the American literary mainstream certainly did their best to foster this myth; but if he was at the time merely a victim of the myths created by others, it is now a crucial tenet of the new consciousness that he is responsible for the myths he must live by, and in this radically altered situation it can no longer be sufficient to argue that white racism is the cause of the persistence of this obviously inadequate species of heroism. Whatever the merits of Mr. Hernton's thesis may be, it seems to us, therefore, necessary to suggest that if our reading of the situation is a plausible one, an alarming condition does in fact exist, that there appears to be a dangerous tendency in black fiction in this country to exaggerate the symbolic significance of sexual heroism, and to deny, in the process, the black woman's nobility, her humanity, and this last in spite of popular claims that she has at long last come to take her place as the true paragon of beauty and grace that she has always been.

The situation in the black creative imagination, as we see it, is certainly more alarming, but we do not mean to suggest that the realities of the popular imagination are any more objectively impeccable or desirable. If our creative writers tend, sometimes unconsciously, to underestimate the significance and importance of the black female, certain portions of the popular black press and other media do compensate enough for this by their often extravagant claims; but if black women were to reflect on what happened, historically, to their white counterparts in this country, they would probably not feel too flattered by Mr. Cleaver's all-too-literary adoration. The white woman in America became both spiritually and sexually enslaved precisely at the point when she allowed herself to be deified by her mate. In exchange for her canonization, she became a frustrated, because oversanctified, curiosity. And it is not without reason that she has become more assertive, and certainly less of a sanctified ornament in these days when her mate is beginning to discover, openly, that beauty or sexual attraction is not coterminous with the accidents of gender, and also that the ultra-feminine female does in fact have limited and non-exclusive sexual uses. If the Essence Magazine type of glorification of the black female were to become a predominant mood in black consciousness, there might well come the day also, when the black woman will seek to be rescued from her canonical strangulation.

On the other hand, the situation, with respect to this problem, is at the present time too fluid to justify any pessimistic prophecies of the rise of a black women's liberation movement which would, in any case, not be so tragic a development. (It is, after all, possible to conceive of a state of affairs in which the black man, having exhausted all the means at his disposal, would be obliged to yield preeminence to the black woman in the struggle for freedom. Consider, for a brief moment, the possible consequences of an event in which forty black *women* are shot down at Attica!) In any case, there is as we shall suggest in a later chapter, one major conclusion that may be derived from Baldwin's own responses to the issue of sexuality in art. In *Go Tell, Giovanni's Room,* and *Another Country,* the sexual 'heroism' of his male characters was primarily characterised by an intensely individualistic (sometimes even anarchistic) search for personal identity that often had little to do with the predominantly communal nature of their social predicament, and it may be argued that at this point Baldwin had as yet not discovered the symbolic uses to which the theme of sexuality could be effectively put. But there is, in his last novel—*Tell Me*—sufficient evidence to suggest that he has now come to see that sexual heroism need not be an individual end in itself, but in fact a powerful symbol of the kind of 'love' upon which committed political action can be based. In other words, it is not at all difficult to conceive of a situation in which the vital energies expended in sexual engagement are directed toward the achievement of more socio-political ends, and if Baldwin's success on this score is less than perfect in *Tell Me*, we have reason to expect a more accomplished treatment of the subject in his later works.

This then, is the agony of blackness, a search for meaningful identity that has led our black writers into sometimes strange, sometimes exhilarating paths. A major intention behind the analysis offered in this chapter has been to suggest, first, that there does exist a black tradition in literature and thought in America to which Baldwin inextricably belongs, and secondly, that the concept of the Black Aesthetic need not be an instrument of exclusion, but one, rather, that makes it possible for us to include in the tradition all those whose minds have in varying ways been exercised by the agony of blackness. We have suggested that this approach need not indeed preclude discriminations and evaluative judgment, but should more positively make it easier to lend sufficient significance to the contributions of all the writers in the tradition. With respect to Baldwin, we have sought primarily to emphasize the ultimately moral interpretation of life that characterised his preliminary vision of blackness, and the limitations of this vision; but it must also be observed that his was a constantly maturing imagination, and that, as we hope to illustrate, his latest works: *Tell Me* and *No Name in the Street*, clearly indicate that a more positively socio-political consciousness is beginning to supercede the moral preoccupations of his earlier writings.

Notes to Chapter Six

1. Norman Mailer, *The Armies of the Night*, Signet, 1968, p. 29
2. See Imamu Braka's sensitive remarks on the distinction between Black American slave songs and the work songs of Africa, in *Blues People*, William Morrow, 1963, pp. 18–19.
3. Ruth Miller, ed., *Black American Literature*, Beverly Hills, 1971, p. 202
4. Quoted in Ruth Miller, op. cit., p. 203
5. Booker T. Washington was in fact much older than Dunbar, though his Atlanta Exposition Address came a few years after the publication of Dunbar's first book of poems.
6. References to McKay's poems are taken from Houston A. Baker, Jr. ed., *Black Literature in America*, McGraw-Hill, 1971, pp. 165–68
7. Baldwin, *Notes of a Native Son*, Bantam, 1964, p. 138
8. Baldwin, 'Princes and Powers,' *Nobody Knows My Name*, Corgi, 1965, p. 29. LeRoi Jones, in *Blues People*, comes to much the same conclusion regarding the transformation of African work songs into slave songs in America.
9. ibid.
10. ibid., pp. 31–32
11. ibid., p. 33
12. Houston Baker, op. cit., p. 241
13. Baldwin, *The Fire Next Time*, p. 132
14. ibid., pp. 132–33
15. Mrs. Collier appears as unaware of this confusion as Baldwin is. See her 'Thematic Patterns in Baldwin's Essays,' *Black World*, June 1972, pp. 28–34
16. See the *New York Times* report on the Conference of the New School for Social Research, Sunday, April 25, 1965.
17. Julian Mayfield, 'And Then Came Baldwin', in John Henrik Clarke, ed., *Harlem, U.S.A.*, East Berlin, Seven Seas, p. 160.

18. Cleaver, op. cit., p. 97 ff.
19. Harold Cruse, *The Crisis of the Negro Intellectual*, Apollo, 1967, p. 496
20. See Addison Gayle, *The Black Aesthetic*, pp. 32–38
21. See Baldwin, *Nobody Knows My Name*, p. 30
22. Ron Karenga, in Gayle, op. cit., p. 33
23. An important objection here would be that this argument does not even begin to grapple with the issue of the precise definition of blackness, even with a lower case 'b.' To this it may be replied, first, that as with 'virtue,' we do have a general idea of what blackness means, even if it is difficult to find a rigorous and useful enough definition of it; and secondly, that since at such a level of definitions one is necessarily involved in the stipulation of arbitrary rules, Ron Karenga's definition appears to us as useful as any, as a means of evaluation and judgment.
24. This is an assumption clearly implicit in Karenga's views on cultural nationalism. See Gayle, op. cit., p. 24.
25. The thesis that passion and violence are inseparable elements in the literature of love in the Western world is a long-standing one, and it would hardly serve any useful purpose here to reiterate the numerous variatons on this theme. A good deal, too, has been written on the various categories of 'Love,' particularly on the distinctions between the erotic and the spiritual; and in dealing here with sexuality in black fiction, we do not mean to claim for it any exclusive characteristics not observable in other fictions. The primary purpose here is one of limited analysis, and though, with respect to black American fiction, we have chosen not to discuss Western literature in general, the broader perspective must be borne in mind. The situation in African fiction is, however, a different one, and its characteristic elements are sufficiently significant to justify the supposition of a separate fictional sensibility. Portions of this chapter were read as a Paper at the Conference on Linkages in the Black Pluriverse, held at the State University of New York at Binghamton in November 1971.
26. Eldridge Cleaver, op. cit., pp. 176–77
27. Richard Wright, *Native Son*, Harper and Row, 1966, p. 219
28. Baldwin, *Another Country*, pp. 16–17
29. See Susan Sontag, *Styles of Radical Will*, p. 66
30. Chinua Achebe, *Things Fall Apart*, Fawcett, 1959, p. 103

Seven

From Allegory to Realism

Another Country was primarily, in intention at any rate, a novel of outrage, one in which its author sought to describe the malignant scope of racial prejudice in American life and the effects it had on the oppressed; but it dealt also with the more general predicament of individual characters, white and black, who sought in their own way and with varying degrees of success to accommodate the pain of their lives. Baldwin's sense of outrage in this novel was convincingly intense, but as we have suggested, he appears to have been undecided as to the precise uses to which anger may legitimately be put. We have seen how anger leads to Rufus' self-destruction and how Ida's fury apparently leads to her final demoralisation; we have also seen how a contemplation of Rufus' and Ida's outrage appears to be instrumental to the regeneration of Eric, Vivaldo and Cass. It is useful here to consider some of the implications of this dramatic situation, especially as it does have far-reaching consequences for the situation in Baldwin's subsequent novel. First, it would probably be doing him an injustice to suppose that he meant here to imply that the anger of the oppressed could in normal circumstances lead to a voluntary determination of the privileged to change the conditions that breed social outrage, for, as he himself was well aware, freedom was not a commodity that was given; it was one that had to be seized by the oppressed. But the situation which Baldwin presents in this novel seemed mistakenly to imply that there was a necessary relation between Rufus' tragedy and the self-discovery of such characters as Cass, Vivaldo and Eric. On the contrary, it would be perfectly plausible to argue that despite their obvious sense of complicity in Rufus' tragedy, if they appear deter-

147

mined to build 'another country,' their motivations are only tangentially related to the sources of Rufus' and Ida's predicament in society, and not directly caused by the latter. The world they anticipate is not a world founded on the principles of political justice, but rather, one whose citizens are bound together by a history of private suffering. If Eric and Vivaldo feel bound to Rufus and Ida, it is not because they recognise a political relationship between themselves and the latter, but rather because they see a *symbolic* link between the nature of their alienation and of Rufus' and Ida's dispossession. Their concerns are not political, but metaphysical, existential, and that Baldwin should thus have postulated their responses as a viable means of resolving the dilemmas of such characters as Rufus and Ida indicated a certain limitation of vision that contributed to the imperfections of *Another Country*. Baldwin was in his next novel to show little interest in this specific issue, but within this context the manner in which he resolves Rufus' and Ida's sense of outrage also indicated a certain confusion regarding responses that are possible and those that are inevitable. In appearing to suggest that suicide and demoralisation inevitably attended social outrage, he mistakenly attached a social significance to individual, psychologically motivated choices that the dramatic situation that he presents could not legitimately justify. It is, of course, possible that despite the potentially explosive political material that Baldwin uses in *Another Country*, the novel was itself not at all a political novel, but it is worth noting here that by the time he wrote his next novel he seems to have succeeded in clarifying his views, at least with respect to the uses of anger in fiction. In any case, one may plausibly argue that a fundamental cause of the imperfections in *Another Country* has to do with the uneasy conflict between the expression of public outrage and the prescription of essentially haphazard, whimsical and individual solutions for the ills of society.

In spite of these confusions and limitations, however, the introduction of a socio-political ambience in *Another Country* was a significant indication of Baldwin's growing concern with social issues, of his gradual movement away from exclusively theological preoccupations. It need hardly be observed that it was precisely because of his concern here with the nature of racial prejudice and its consequences that his New York novel became so powerful an indictment of injustice in society, and it is for this reason that *Another Country* persists in our memory less for its formal, structural achievements than for the intensity of its fury. Anger performs, then, a useful redeeming function in *Another Country*, attesting to a vitality of sensibility, if not a clarity of thought, that distinguishes this novel from his earlier works. But when we come to his latest fictional effort, *Tell Me How Long the Train's Been Gone*, we begin to suspect that the psychic effort the former novel demanded was an almost devastating one—one too, that could, apparently not be sustained (the harrowing and catastrophic events of the sixties must have contributed, also, to the mood of this novel). The achievements of *Tell Me* are of a different order from those of the former novel. Despite Baldwin's return in his latest novel to the lyric mood of his earlier writings, *Tell Me* reads, finally, like the testament of a tired, exhausted mind, an apology for a certainly eventful but nonetheless less than memorable life. And we say this not merely because the narrator of the story is, for the first time in Baldwin's works, middle-aged, nor because he is suffering from a possibly terminal disease, but primarily because, though he is by no means an old man, he appears to have reached a point in his life beyond which everything is mere repetition. We may, indeed, tentatively observe at this point that one of the things that keeps this novel moving is the narrator's desperate search for a faith, an idea that has sufficient vital energy to tide him over the rest of his days. Leo Proudhammer, the narrator of the events in this novel, is not only physically exhausted, but the language he uses, his recollections of things past, is couched in the terminology of profound fatigue. Every significant event in the story happens in the past, before, that is, Leo's prostration by a heart attack. And it is important at this point to emphasize the not insignificant role that 'memory' serves in this novel. Memory, the evocation of an imperfectly consummated life, is not an exercise that is engaged in here in any apparent tranquility; Leo Proudhammer clearly does not, through an exercise of memory, achieve the spiritual peace of the Wordsworthian bard. If anything, the more Leo looks back on his life, the more he apologetically recalls the fits and starts, the tortuous and indirect crooked ways, the compromises he has had to make to become what he is, a famed black actor in a profession dominated by whites. Nevertheless, if, despite this sense of pervasive fatigue that we have, we suspect any residual vitality in Leo, it is precisely because of the apologies he has to make for his life, the justifications he is compelled to offer. And it is in this regard that the remembrance of things past may be seen to serve in this novel the same kind of structural function that anger performs in *Another Country*. In other words, memory in *Tell Me* provides a certain ordering of an otherwise chaotic experience, and within this search for order we find the ultimate justification, the most persuasive apology that Leo has to offer for his life. In a sense, it does not really matter that we find the paternal link which Leo sees between himself and Christopher rather precious or that we do not see in their relationship any clear causal link between the 'love' that Leo gives and the healthily aggressive personality that Christopher develops at the end of the story. There is little compelling reason to believe that Leo's somewhat ambiguous friendship was essential for the nurturing of Christopher's revolutionary temper; yet it seems plausible to suggest that it is because Leo *believes* in this causal link that any degree of real tension is developed in this novel. For despite Barbara's quite significant role in the story, the focal point of the novel is not to be found in the miseries of interracial love, nor in the price that Leo has to pay for daring to succeed in a racist universe. The fundamental issue in *Tell Me* revolves, rather, around the meaning of the relationship between Leo and Christopher, and the tension in this relationship arises from the conflict that we recognise between Leo's determination to justify his life by taking credit for Christopher's 'birth' and the consideration that this determination appears to come from Leo's uneasy suspicion that his life may have been ultimately meaningless in spite of all his worldly success. Barbara does express Leo's own desperate search for faith when she refers to her own participation in Christopher's birth:

I think we have done something very rare . . . I think we have managed to redeem something. I think it's our love that we redeemed. Who could have guessed such a thing? Black Christopher! [1]

Clearly, there is a sense in which one may see Leo as standing 'in loco parentis' with Christopher; clearly, too, one may in fact see Christopher as deriving a certain minimum of psychic sustenance from this obviously symbolic familial relationship. But what impresses us most here is not so much this specific aspect of their union as the suspicion that the relationship is itself a disturbingly and mutually parasitic one. As we shall see later, it is probably in the nature of the thing itself that Christopher should appear to selfishly exploit Leo at the same time as he dreams of a revolutionary, and therefore communal, resolution of the racial dilemma. And Leo himself, despite his obvious paternal concern for Christopher, clearly rejoices in the opportunity the latter gives him both for reliving his own youthful dreams and for discovering some useful apology for his life. Perhaps this is the stuff out of which true love is fashioned, but it is because of the ambiguity surrounding the essential meaning of this relationship that Leo, in spite of his desperate need to believe that he and Barbara have helped give birth to a radiant hope, is yet uncertain as to the ultimate value of such a birth. It is not altogether surprising therefore that Leo's inclination to acquiesce in Barbara's verdict is yet underscored by a reluctance to believe that his has been an entirely selfless and meaningful labour of love. Observing Christopher from the platform as he sits waiting to make one of his numerous speeches in aid of the movement for racial justice, he reflects upon his role and that of his generation, and wonders if they have in fact done anything useful to protect Christopher and others like him:

I watched Christopher's face. He trusted none of the people with whom I was sitting. Most of them were from five to ten years older than I, and from ten to twenty years older than Christopher. And nothing we had done, or left undone, had been able to save him. [2]

151

The fundamental theme in *Tell Me* revolves, then, not around the effort to describe the details of oppression—a theme which Baldwin had quite exhausted in his essays and earlier novels—but around the progression from allegorical, and therefore ambiguous, rebellion to actual embattlement. For one thing, it is in *Tell Me* that we first find in Baldwin's works the introduction of a positively activist mood. The difference between John Grimes and Christopher is not merely one of characterization but also a difference in philosophical assumptions. John's response in *Go Tell*, though perfectly conceivable as a response to oppression, is nevertheless a rather quixotic one. Confronted with a theological terror that manifests itself in the triadic malice of God, his earthly father and white society, his choice is first to convert the very act of religious worship into a vehicle of deliberate apostasy, and finally to see the possibilities of his 'redemption' primarily in terms of the varieties of vengeance which a fertile imagination offers. In other words, anger does not, in *Go Tell*, bear with it the compulsion to remove, by positive action, its basic causes. John may be painfully aware of the conglomerate menace that threatens to dehumanize him, but the only resolution he appears capable of recognising is the imaginative choice he actually makes of dreaming of the day when he will have the power to crush those who oppress him. As a creative solution to the problem presented in the novel, Baldwin's choice is clearly adequate enough, for John's symbolic rebellion bears within its very ambiguity the attraction of unlimited potential, in terms, that is, of the actual direction in which the rebellion could be particularized. But there is no escaping the consideration that his choice has only a limited practical value, nor that it fails to grapple fully with the issue of how precisely to remove, in practice, the causes of his despair. Baldwin was himself aware, it seems, that the vision presented in this novel was a very tentative one, that *Go Tell* was successful less for the effectiveness of the solutions it prescribes for its protagonist than for the lyric intensity with which it describes John's tragic predicament.

The enormity and ramifications of this predicament were such in fact that Baldwin appears to have felt the need to delineate it beyond the scope of a single novel; it was in a way a form of exorcism by evocation. Where, in *Go Tell*, he employed his theological terror as a paradigm of his hero's social dispossession, *Another Country* was memorable less for its eerily mystical vision than for the searing fury of his evocation of the details of this dispossession. In neither of these novels, however, did he primarily concern himself with anything like a programmatic approach to the issue of resolving the problem of social injustice. Indeed, where John Grimes was at least willing to conceive of the possibility of 'salvation,' if only in a symbolic sense, Rufus, in Baldwin's third novel is so enervated by his suffering that he sees no way out but to take his own life, if with a curse on his lips. It is useful, of course, to observe that as possibilities the choices which John and Rufus make are perfectly plausible and 'realistic' (it should not be difficult to document these in terms of the actual history of black people in this country). What is of greater significance is the consideration that by the time he came to write his latest novel, Baldwin had undergone a crucial conversion; Black Christopher is in all essential respects as far removed from Rufus as Leo Proudhammer is from Richard, the suicide in *Go Tell*. The essence of this development derives from the variety of uses to which anger may be put. In *Go Tell*, it is sublimated into an impalpable and all-embracing rebellion; in *Another Country* it serves as the means by which, ironically, Rufus makes his choice of escaping pain through suicide. By the time we get to *Tell Me* anger is no longer merely an apparently immutable condition, an end in itself, or the source of demoralisation; it no longer leads inescapably to frustration, but rather becomes the very justification for Christopher's positive commitment to specific, programmatic action. It is true, of course, that as in *The Fire Next Time*, this commitment to action is by no means sufficiently delineated; a program of revolutionary engagement is more insinuated than clearly described, but insinuation is in itself a measure of Baldwin's painful movement away from the days when Rufus' suicide appeared to him to be a sufficiently meaningful key to the meaning of life.

The movement away from allegory into 'realism,' indicated by the crucial difference between Rufus and Christopher, is further illustrated by the way in which the homosexual hero, who in earlier novels appeared to possess merely the potential for transforming the world, becomes in *Tell Me* the actual agent of this transformation. All through Baldwin's fictional works, the homosexual character had always been seen as the authentic symbol both of theological and secular rebellion. We have seen how, in *Go Tell*, John's relationship with Elisha is essentially presented as an act of defiance against God; both in the wrestling incident in the Temple of God, and in the final scene of the novel where Elisha rescues John from the abyss of guilt, one meaning of the novel revolves around the rebellious, and therefore (in Baldwin's construct) transforming potential of the homosexual interest. But this interest had always been at once a celebration of freedom as it was attended also by a certain uneasiness arising from the homosexual's sense of dissociation from received morality. And so, in *Giovanni's Room*, what impresses us most is not so much David's celebration of his freedom as his fear that he is fated to suffer God's vengeance. In *Another Country*, it began to be clear that Baldwin's treatment of the homosexual theme was becoming bolder, for it was in this novel that he tried, without much success, to present the homosexual hero (as represented by Eric) as the one single individual capable of founding that country in which, presumably, there would be no injustice. But as we suggested in the preceding chapter, this was not a particularly convincing vision, partly because Baldwin appeared to be more concerned with the salvation of individual souls than with the health of society. With respect to the homosexual theme, therefore, the distinguishing quality of *Tell Me* is precisely this, that Leo is no longer preoccupied with the problem of sin, and that Baldwin appears to present him as the direct source of Christopher's *positive and specific commitment to social action.* Furthermore, whereas in the earlier novels homosexuality was presented as being particularly useful as a symbol of heroic rebellion because it was not procreative (and therefore not brutish or vile) its fundamental value in this novel comes from a contrary viewpoint, namely, that it is indeed eminently 'procreative.' As Leo remarks,

The incestuous brother and sister would now never have any children. But perhaps we had given one child to the world, or helped to open the world to one child. Luckier lovers hadn't managed so much.[3]

Though Leo's immediate reference in the passage above is to the love relationship between him and Barbara, her contribution to Christopher's birth is purely incidental, hers having been rather in the nature of a midwife's role. The significance of this confession is therefore not to be limited to an assertion of the values of interracial heterosexual love—since Christopher is in fact not *their* child—but must be seen to indicate Baldwin's new belief in the procreative potential of homosexuality. But what is of ultimate significance is the consideration that what was presented in the earlier novels mainly as allegory, as paradigm, is in *Tell Me*, offered openly and with much less diffidence as reality. Homosexuality becomes in fact, and not merely in potential, the authentic well-spring of a burgeoning revolutionary mood.

More than a decade before the publication of *Tell Me*, Baldwin had stated in the introduction to his first collection of essays, a number of attitudes and opinions which we legitimately consider to have represented his philosophy at the time. There is hardly any doubt now that at this time he had been more willing to recognise a formal distinction between his life as a social being and his role as an artist. For him it then seemed, art was ambiguity, complex, iconoclastic, heretical, whereas to be a man, especially a black man in America, often demanded a degree of simplification and dogmatism in thought and behaviour that appeared to defeat the very function of art:

Any writer, I suppose, feels that the world into which he was born is nothing less than a conspiracy against the cultivation of his talent—which attitude certainly has a great deal to support it. On the other hand, it is only because the world looks on his talent with such a frightening indifference that the artist is compelled to make his talent important. So that any writer, looking back over even so short a span of time as I am here forced to assess (Baldwin was about thirty at this point) finds that the things which hurt him and the things which help him cannot be divorced from each other; he could be helped in a certain way only because he was hurt in a certain way; and his help is simply to be enabled to move from one conundrum to the next—one is tempted to say that he moves from one disaster to the next.[4]

An important distinction in this view of art was the presumption that art did not demand any kind of meaningful action from its devotees except in so far as this was an intrinsic part of the work of art itself:

> Social affairs are not generally speaking the writer's prime concern, whether they ought to be or not; it is absolutely necessary that he establish between himself and these affairs a distance which will allow, at least, for clarity, so that before he can look forward in any meaningful sense, he must first be allowed to take a long look back.[5]

Baldwin certainly did have enough time to have a long look back, but even a cursory examination of the historical context in which these views were expressed should make it clear that they were by no means peculiar to him. The fifties were after all, the tepid years in American literary history, the years in which it was perfectly possible, if not indeed mandatory, to insist upon the Hemingway-esque distinction between an 'honest man' and a 'good writer' without being scoffed at. The irony in this situation was, however, an exquisitely intriguing one; for, those who like Baldwin, thought that their advocacy of the autonomy of art came from their own pure philosophical disquisitions seemed blissfully unaware that the very concept they embraced was basically little more than a defensive response to prevalent *political* conditions in American culture. It is hardly necessary here to adjudicate the validity of this view of art. It is more useful to observe that by the time Baldwin conceived of the character of Black Christopher and his relationship to Leo Proudhammer, he had moved far away from the days, more than a decade before, when his primary ambition appeared to have been to achieve eminence as 'a writer.'

If John Grimes continues to have any claim on our attention, it is both because we recall the enormity of his predicament and because, also, we are persuaded to accept that by virtue of his imaginative sensibility, which is of course the generic realm of the artist, he is capable of triumphing over his condition in a manner not allowed to ordinary mortals. Baldwin's fictional works are replete with artist-characters—men whose deep sensitivity both more deeply exposes them to the malice of their community and yet allows them a degree of perception whereby they come up with the proper, if sometimes tragic responses. Richard, again in *Go Tell*, is the artist's prototype, a man who rather than accommodate evil, leaves the world by taking his own life. Rufus, in *Another Country* is another example of the significance which Baldwin was accustomed to lend to the exclusive sensitivity of the artist. But though they may be just as prone to it as other less endowed mortals, not all artists were willing to capitulate to the suicidal dictates of their sensitivity, and so, in *Another Country*, Eric is the artist *par excellence,* the man who, being only too aware of the world's 'conspiracy against the cultivation of his talent,' prefers not to remove himself from life, but rather to erect around himself a new world, divorced from ours, in which its citizens rather self-consciously worship before the altar of pain and suffering. Action, then, is for these earlier artist figures in Baldwin, objectionable, especially if it took into account the political ambience of their lives. And it is a measure of Baldwin's development that in *Tell Me*, Leo Proudhammer is even willing to give speeches at public rallies despite his own misgivings, while a character like Eric would be literally devastated by any such appearance that was not absolutely anonymous. It is not that Leo ceases to be an artist once he recognises the possibility of becoming a man; at the end of his recuperation he does return to work in the theatre, but it is quite clear also that once his mask is removed following his heart attack, its very removal indicates a positive conversion, for it is at that point that he "gets his own face back" and begins to see the possibility of participation, however vicarious, in the life of those around him.[6]

Furthermore, at the risk of undue forays in the realm of 'interpretation,' it is useful to suggest that the hospital to which Leo is taken serves an essential structural function in the novel. It is there

that he finds both the time and the need for reflection, and the outcome of his meditations is his discovery that, whether by accident
or by design, he has helped bring a new hope into the world in the
person of Black Christopher. The ambiguities of response are still
there in his thoughts, the almost compulsive search for complexities, but the mask is gone, and what we finally have is a vision of
the artist as political man, still reluctant to commit himself categor-
ically to public action, but willing nevertheless to concede the legitimacy of Christopher's view of the world. It can hardly be overem-
phasized that this development was a crucial one for Baldwin,
partly the consequence, no doubt, of the different mood of the sixties, but fundamentally the result of his own recognition that it was
by no means a necessary and sufficient condition of success that
the artist's responsibility should end with the lyric expression of
anger or with the search for ambiguity in life. Ultimately, therefore,
Leo's final declaration of commitment at the end of his story—

> . . . when the shit hit the fan, I wanted to be at the wire with
> them—not, being black like them, that I flattered myself about
> having any choice . . .

must be seen for what it clearly is, a blunt if less than eloquent indication of Baldwin's own discovery of a new perspective on life.

Another implication of this new perspective has to do with Leo's
renunciation of God. In the context of the development we have
sought to delineate, the rise to primacy in Baldwin's thought of the
secular city implied the disappearance of his preoccupation with
the 'theophobic' matrix. We have argued that when John Grimes is
'saved' in *Go Tell*, his salvation is in practical terms a somewhat un-
availing one for the very reason that he is still caught within a cosmology in which one either served God and led a frustrated, un-
fulfilled life here on earth, or one renounced Him and forever lived
with the fear of damnation. If, as we also suggested, we see David's
role in *Giovanni's Room* as an extension of John's predicament in
the earlier novel, it becomes clear that John's salvation can only
lead to David's uneasy freedom, precisely because the two characters are trapped, despite their inclination toward rebellion and her-

esy, within a view of the world in which reality appears almost exclusively to be expressed as a set of theological propositions. By the same token, Rufus' final curse in *Another Country* appears curiously appropriate; he renounces God *because* he fears Him, and having done this his only recourse is to remove himself, he thinks, from the scope of God's vengeance by committing suicide. In other words, so long as Baldwin remained a victim of theological terror, his preoccupations were bound to be primarily spiritual, even mystical. The implausible utopia of which Eric is a founding spirit in *Another Country* does not essentially therefore, reflect the type of secular concern which we find in *Tell Me*. Eric's new world, as we argued earlier, is at worst a world of the mind, and at best an attempt to bring the city of God down here on earth. It is inconceivable that such a city could be equipped to deal with the socio-political problems that Baldwin's own description of the real world implies, and we therefore leave the world of this novel perhaps obsessively impressed by its fury, but unable in any practical way to find some cathartic mitigation of our complicity in such a hideous world.

In a sense, then, what Baldwin does in *Tell Me* is precisely to offer us this opportunity for mitigation. One does not have to agree with the particular resolution he presents to recognise the plausibility of it all. Through Leo Proudhammer he suggests to us the limits of individual effort. Leo's life has not been an idyllic one; he had had to bear infinite indignities in order to become a success in his profession, and in a sense, of course, his own personal triumph over prejudice is no doubt meant to suggest to us that Rufus' choice in *Another Country* is not an ineluctable one. Further, because of his own personal achievement, he has been obliged to make some contribution, in money and personal appearances, toward the movement for justice in society. But his very success, coupled with his own sense of the complexity of the issues involved, does help to alienate him from his community, and as Christopher quite bluntly puts it, his integrity is now in question:

> You want to know if they still love you in the streets—you want to know what they think of you . . . A whole lot of cats dig you, and some of them love you. But, Leo, you a fat cat now. That's

the way a whole lot of people see you, and you can't blame them, how *else* can they see you. And we in a situation where we have to know which people we can trust, which people we can use— that's the nitty-gritty.[7]

Leo, of course, never quite reaches Christopher's heights of proud and determined affirmation (he is in fact not required to) but he does achieve a degree of fraternal sympathy that leads him to see the justification, if not the necessity, of Christopher's cause. And the fundamental point to be made here is that to reach this level of awareness and sympathy, Leo had first to rid himself of the theophobic matrix which had in earlier novels led Baldwin's characters to different choices. The affirmation of the secular city, as even youthful Christopher clearly sees, demands not, to be sure, a renunciation of the sacred (for Christopher's is in all practical terms a religious commitment) but a renunciation of 'God.' When Rufus curses God in *Another Country*, his is a last desperate gasp of defiance, but his defiance does not bring with it deliverance from fear, but leads him rather to the tragic denial of life. When Leo, on the other hand, denounces Caleb's God, he does recognise that deliverance comes only through the determination to go on living. To insist on life is to be 'political.' And so when Leo cries out against Caleb and his God, we are required to see this denunciation not simply as an expression of impotent fury, but primarily as an indication of a crucial point of departure in Baldwin's fictions:

Once, I wanted to be like you . . . I would have given anything in the world to be like you . . . Now I'd rather die than be like you. I wouldn't be like you and tell all these lies, to all these ignorant people, all these unhappy people, for anything in the world, Caleb, anything in the world! That God you talk about, that miserable white cock-sucker—look at his handiwork, look! I curse your God, Caleb, I curse Him, from the bottom of my heart I curse Him. And now let Him strike me down. Like you just tried to do.[8]

160

It is not without significance that the rhythm of this denunciation is the rhythm of ritual. The incantatory tone is deliberate because Leo's is a formal declaration of separation.

It is worth emphasizing that from this point on, Baldwin appears to have come to see that though the choices that such earlier characters as John, Rufus and Eric make may have been plausible, there was yet nothing inevitable in their responses. Indeed, the very choices that they make derive from Baldwin's own apparent belief that the essential quality in the dilemma of twentieth century man was its *privacy*, and that only private responses were adequate for confronting it. It was a belief that his own personal history was in many respects only too apt an illustration. But changing conditions in the sixties no doubt convinced him that the black man's burden, at any rate, was hardly an individual one, and it became therefore mandatory for a writer as honest as Baldwin sought to be, to find a different set of solutions for a dilemma he now saw from a different perspective. From *Another Country* to *Tell Me*, Baldwin had passed from a vision in which he appeared to see life as a matter of private myth-making to one in which public action had become all-important. From allegory he had moved toward realism; from myth he began to search for an understanding of contemporary history.

To dwell upon the significance of this conceptual development is, however, not at the same time to suggest that the structural framework Baldwin employed was entirely adequate. Essentially, the story is Christopher's story, but the structure of the novel revolves around Leo. The rise of Black Christopher is the single most important aspect of the novel that justifies its being the crucial development that distinguishes *Tell Me* from Baldwin's earlier novels; yet, despite the scattered notices we have of Christopher's origins and dreams, and despite what we see as the author's clear intention to celebrate this promise, the sheer bulk of the novel deals, nevertheless, with the processes by which Leo is enabled to renounce the cosmology of fear and affirm the hope that Christopher brings with him. It is not, however, simply a matter of the amount of space the author devotes to the two components of his vision in this novel; it is rather a question of structural emphasis, but, as in *Another Coun-*

try, the flaw in *Tell Me* has basically to do with the manner in which Baldwin appears determined to detract our attention from the true meaning of his story. Where the former novel was a dirge of anger, *Tell Me* is intrinsically a celebration of the rise of the authentic black man, confident, proud, determined and religiously committed to life. But just as in *Another Country* Baldwin moved beyond the effective end of his story, namely, the history of Rufus' life and suicide, and presented us with an ill-conceived vision of utopia, so also in *Tell Me* he diverts our attention from the real interest of the story, namely, Christopher's rise and promise, and dwells rather indulgently upon a diagnosis of Leo's less than heroic inadequacies.

It is tempting, of course, to argue that the failure of moral energy is at the root of this persistent obfuscation in Baldwin's fictions, that there is in his sensibility a curious abhorrence of non-cerebral action. But whatever the truth of the matter, the one thing that is clear is that the process of development that gave birth to Black Christopher was a prolonged and often painful one for James Baldwin. The distinctive achievement of *Tell Me* is that in spite of its structural flaws, it does attempt to offer us a synthesis of the themes in the Baldwin corpus. We have seen how the theme of theological terror runs through his works, from his early essay on Mrs. Stowe's novel to Rufus' curse in *Another Country*. The obsession with damnation was one that Baldwin had to exorcise before he could begin to dwell upon more secular themes. But the ritual of exorcism was not a simple matter of renunciation. It was a slow and painful process that began with John's symbolic rebellion in *Go Tell*, through David's discovery in ·*Giovanni's Room* that his merely intellectual awareness of dissociation from God did not necessarily rid him of his more visceral, psychic sense of corruption; from this point Baldwin moved on to examine Rufus' more socio-political dispossession, one that was founded, as he saw it, upon the Judaeo-Christian ethic of racial superiority. In this context, Rufus' cry against God was a perfectly natural response to his misery, but Baldwin must have been aware that the suicide that follows this cry, though plausible as a behavioural response, was yet questionable as a useful means of confronting one's social dilemma. In other words, a rhetorical denunciation of God was meaningless unless one were capable of evolving an alternative cosmology, a different way of looking at life. It is in this regard that the rise of Black Christopher in *Tell Me* indicated a crucial turning point in Baldwin's career. For, not only does this character not possess any of the theophobic neuroses of the earlier figures, his commitment to the politics of active confrontation also underscores his belief in the essential worth of man.

Another issue with which Baldwin had for long been preoccupied is that of how effectively to present the homosexual as an authentic instrument of change in society. We have argued that the essential meaning of John's relationship with Elisha lies in Baldwin's diffident attempt to subvert the ritual of Christian worship; we have seen also how the significance of Eric's role in *Another Country* lies primarily in the potential he is shown as possessing for transforming the world by virtue of his homosexual inclinations. It was not, however, till *Tell Me* that Baldwin was able to discover a structural framework capable of appropriating the procreative principle of heterosexuality and thereby 'giving birth' to Black Christopher. At this point it may be said that Baldwin had 'solved' the problem of homosexuality by making it an intrinsic part of Christopher's revolutionary commitment.

By the same token, the movement away from the vision of man as 'homo theologicus' is paralleled by the dethronement from preeminence of art and the artist. It is not without reason that all the earlier characters in Baldwin are artists or men with what might vaguely be termed an artistic sensibility—John, Rufus, David (to a lesser degree), Eric, and Leo. The artist in Baldwin is a man profoundly aware of the complexities of life, suspicious of action and the simplified justifications of action, unwilling to embrace any ideologies though deeply aware of the pain and tragedy of life, and, finally, preoccupied with evolving a *private* strategy of survival. Not until *Tell Me* was the artist to emerge from his private world (if only grudgingly, as Leo does) and finally show some willingness to concede the value of involvement and yield his preeminence to a political protagonist as undisturbed by complexities as Christopher is. What Baldwin's artists had done was to internalize their anger and consequently fail to see that their sense of outrage could in fact become a creative instrument of revolutionary and therefore communal engagement. The political protagonist, on the other hand, was not satisfied merely with *feeling;* sensitivity was not for him an end in itself, nor was it a vehicle of alienation from those others who also felt and suffered the way the protagonist did. Rather, to feel and to be hurt was a necessary condition for meaningful and committed action on behalf of fellow travellers in pain. That Baldwin finally came to this realisation is a clear indication of his continued growth as a writer, and it is a development that justifies us in the belief that at forty-eight, he is still too young to have reached the point where he no longer has anything meaningful to say to his readers.

Notes to Chapter Seven

1. Baldwin, *Tell Me How Long the Train's Been Gone*, Dell, 1968, p. 80
2. ibid., p. 84
3. ibid., p. 336
4. Baldwin, 'Autobiographical Notes,' *Notes of a Native Son*, Bantam, 1955, p. 2
5. ibid., pp. 3–4
6. Baldwin, *Tell Me*, p. 9
7. ibid., pp. 366–67
8. ibid., p. 326

Eight

Conclusion

We have argued that any meaningful interpretation of Baldwin's writings to date would have to take into consideration his need to exorcise his private dread of hell, a dread he inherited from his childhood and adolescent involvement in the store-front churches of Harlem. There is hardly any doubt at this time either of the immensity of this dread, or, as we shall suggest in a moment, of the intrinsic significance it has had for his works. His early relationship to the church in Harlem has always been both a limitation and spur to the flowering of his creative talent: a limitation, because in terms of the development of a sufficiently realistic vision of life, it for a long time constituted a near insurmountable obstacle to his discovery of an authentic public voice; and an inspiration, because, in terms of the aesthetic sufficiency of his writings, he was always at his best when he was content to delineate the scope of his peculiar private inheritance. In other words, despite their tendency to dwell on a somewhat rarefied experience, *Go Tell* and *Giovanni's Room* are, in terms of the coalescence in them of form and content, much better works than both *Another Country* and *Tell Me*. The two latter novels, on the other hand, though clearly less perfect as finished creative artifacts, do have a degree of seriousness around them that distinguishes them as works bearing greater public significance than Baldwin's first two novels. And it is on the strength of this last consideration that we feel justified in speculating that he will be remembered less for his technical achievements as a novelist than for the degree of passion which he has brought to a creative examination of public issues.

There is a certain dialectic at work in the Baldwin corpus. So long as he chose to guide us on a tour of his own private hell, the structural means he employed tended to be quite adequate for the limited purposes they were intended to serve. One would hardly be justified in suggesting that there is in the early novels anything like aesthetically satisfying form without much meaningful content, yet there is the consideration also that especially in *Giovanni's Room*, the limits of Baldwin's concerns do border rather close on capricious whimsy. It is not that an examination of the theological implications of 'the humanist heresy' (in the case of *Giovanni's Room*, of homosexual liberation) is in itself trivial or insignificant, but the significance of such an examination ultimately derives precisely from its implications for man in society. David's anxiety to convince himself that he is actually free and that he may insist on his freedom without the fear of damnation may be for him a perfectly crucial and all-important problem, but it is also necessary to remark, at the risk of implying any specific or dogmatic 'ends' for art, that the 'problem' would probably not exist, and if it did, would certainly not be worth examining were he in fact an isolated being. Yet quite often we observe David (and Giovanni a little less so) acting as though Paris were an unpopulated city inhabited only by two solitary, historyless and reluctant heretics, and this in spite of all the cumulatively oppressive evidence to the contrary. It is not, in a word, the validity of David's predicament that is in question, but its significance. And it is this early reluctance on Baldwin's part to clearly connect the admittedly real psychological vexations of individual characters to their origins in the cultural fabric of their societies that we refer to when we suggest that his early novels lacked sufficiently serious, meaningful content.

Despite the conceptual limitations of Baldwin's first two novels, and his somewhat obsessive preoccupation with his own private world, there can be little doubt now that this preoccupation was in itself an indispensable, if not mandatory, exercise in self-therapy. In a sense, indeed, Baldwin had become, technically, a 'writer' long before he found anything to write about—anything, that is, that went beyond an embellished autobiography—and self-therapy was required precisely because he had to cease, as it were, to be a writer before he could find a subject-matter and a voice. (The last remark is not intended as facetious witticism. Anyone familiar with the rhetorical foundations of the Black Ministry in this country will readily admit that the profession of preaching is one of the best training grounds for a would-be writer. The complicated synthesis of down-to-earth homilies and biblical exempla, buttressed by an engaging core of personal testimony was, and still is, a most useful exercise for anyone who wished to acquire the technique of writing fiction.)[1] Baldwin, in short, acquired his sense of form from his apprenticeship in evangelical oratory, but from it also he inherited a sense of private theological danger, a cosmology based on an awesomely invidious divine contract, primarily distinguished by man's unequal relationship to God rather than his equal relationship to other men in society.

Confronted with this ambiguous inheritance, it is conceivable of course that Baldwin could deliberately have chosen permanently to remain within the confines of this cosmology, in which case he would have continued to produce works like *Go Tell* and *Giovanni's Room* in which his characters are for ever driven either into cowering submission or into schizophrenic heresy by their sense of sin. In this case, also, he would presumably have continued to present us with works as technically competent as *Go Tell* but as equally questionable in terms of the seriousness of their themes. But he chose to travel another road, partly driven by the logic of events, and primarily motivated by the exigencies of his own private vision of life. He must have realised that the age of the divine order of things was long gone, that we now lived in a world in which social behaviour was no longer reducible to theological disquisitions on sin and virtue. To effectively testify to this recognition, he had first to rid himself of his psychic enslavement to the cosmology of damnation, and his first two novels may legitimately, therefore, be seen as therapeutic rituals of exorcism in which the very act of confrontation with theological dreads bears within itself the potential for destroying these fears. By the time he conceived the character of Rufus, who first curses God and then commits suicide, it was clear that the tension in Baldwin between a theology of fear and a more secular vision was beginning to resolve itself—a process of resolution that was to become more apparent both in the character of Black Christopher in *Tell Me* and in Baldwin's most recent essay, *No Name in the Street*. Unfortunately, however, it would appear that the price he has had to pay for his furious passage from the realms of theological terror to the outskirts of the secular city has been a loss of that masterly control of form and structure that one could observe in his earlier, less ambitious novels.[2]

To raise the issue of structure in a discussion of Baldwin is to expose oneself to objections from two mutually incompatible camps: the New Novelists and the advocates of the Black Aesthetic in art. The former would presumably object that if *Another Country* and *Tell Me* are less perfect artistic wholes than his earlier novels, the reason for this does not lie in the inadequacies of plot and structure, on the grounds that the concept of 'structure' is an outmoded, bourgeois value that disappeared with the decline of the 'rationalistic order'.[3] Some advocates of the Black Aesthetic would, on the other hand, dismiss any discussions of 'structure' out of hand, not, as in the case of the New Novelists, on the basis of any specific aesthetic or philosophical objections, but mainly because the concept of structure is thought to be the brainchild of a dying Western culture.[4] One implication of this last position is, apparently, the supposition that 'the idea of structure'—the close and effective link between the idea-content of a work of art and the means by which this is presented—is one that is foreign to black art. This, in our opinion, is a mistaken view of the situation. As we have already suggested, the effective control of 'form' was and still is a crucial rhetorical equipment of the Black Minister (consider, for instance, Martin Luther King's 'Letter from Birmingham Jail,' a 'letter' whose exquisite form is unquestionable) and is an acquisition that one can hardly trace back to the rhetorical counsels of Cicero or Quintilian. More fundamental, however, is the consideration that despite the countless 'functionalist' interpretations of African art that abound, it is not often seen that the recognition of a specific function in an African work of art presupposes an antecedent obligation on the part of the artist himself to employ only those means that are adequate and necessary for the discharge of a particular function. To talk about 'means' is to talk about plot and form and the relationship of these to meaning. One is not obliged in an essay

168

such as this to respond to the mystifications of a novelist like Robbe-Grillet, which may or may not have significance depending on the kind of literature one is dealing with; but it does appear necessary to dispose of the myth that a discussion of such issues as structure and form is inimical to the spirit of Black Literature. A basic structural flaw in *Another Country* lies, not in the description of the environment of Rufus' despair, nor in the presentation of his response to this environment. It derives, rather, from Baldwin's failure to convincingly relate this to the vaguely realised utopian dream that informs the latter part of this novel. We are not at all persuaded, that is to say, that Eric's reluctant and apparently unconscious evangelism is clearly presented as having a demonstrable connection with Rufus' predicament, nor is it clear to us that that 'other country' which Baldwin anticipates with Yves' arrival in New York is at all qualitatively designed to transcend, let alone transform, the evils of Rufus' world. By the same token, the basic flaw in *Tell Me* has to do, as we have argued, with Baldwin's failure to lend sufficient emphasis to the advent of Black Christopher, the promise which his arrival implied, and the clearly crucial shift which this meant for Baldwin's vision of the world. To say, therefore, that these two novels are structurally imperfect is to say in a different language what one would mean if one said that an old Senegalese Griot was a bad story-teller.

We do not wish to belabour the issue here, but we do insist that even in terms specifically of African and Afro-American Art, it would be quite difficult to talk meaningfully about 'function' without at the same time raising fundamental questions of plot, form and structure. In the case of Baldwin, what seems to have happened is that he had gradually begun to alter the idea-content of his writing without making allowances for certain necessary changes in the fictional forms that were meant to convey these ideas. The sermonic style of the Black Ministry was ideally suited for personal testimony, for the conveyance of emotion, faith and passion, of non-secular, non-analytical verities.[5] The strength and success of his earlier novels, as of most of his essays, depended precisely on his ability to make their content serve the intention of creating heightened feeling in his readers, often without the aid of 'consecu-

169

tive reasoning.' The later novels, on the other hand, by the very nature of their subject-matter, required a greater exercise of analytical power, a greater coherence between causes and their effects, between the psychological motivations of individual characters and the social canvas on which they acted out their lives. Baldwin succeeded in these novels in proportion to his ability to achieve this coherence. Objectively considered, the structural imperfections of *Another Country* and *Tell Me* may simply be considered as failures of craft, but one may also speculate on the psychological causes of this failure. First, if one saw his movement from an ambiguous love-hate relationship toward the Eternal City to an albeit hesitant affirmation of the need to come to terms with the secular city as a process of development in time, it would be easier to see these structural faults as provisional imperfections. One would therefore be justified in speculating that his next novel will be an altogether more accomplished one than *Tell Me*. Secondly, it seems clear now that he has been unduly suspicious that what often passes for intellectualism in art is a cloak for aridity of feeling. He is not alone in this suspicion of course, but what it has meant for his work is an often troubled hesitation before the exigencies of logical inevitability. 'I refuse to believe' is a phrase he is accustomed to use rather often, a clear indication of his own desire to transcend humdrum determinisms. More fundamental, however, to an understanding of these hesitations is the consideration that Baldwin's sense of privacy, his faith in the primacy of the individual life, has always been quite pronounced. Even as recently as his latest essay, which is in mood and focus appreciably less emotional and more analytical than his earlier ones, we get the impression that what once was an article of faith is in the process of being converted into a philosophical truth:

> But I think that it is just as well to remember that the people are one mystery and that the person is another. Though I know what a very bitter and delicate and dangerous conundrum this is, it yet seems to me that a failure to respect the person so dangerously limits one's perception of the people that one risks betraying them and oneself, either by sinking to the apathy of cynical dis-

appointment, or rising to the rage of knowing better than the people do, what the people want.[6]

The point to be made here then is that this powerful sense of the primacy of the person does have far-reaching consequences for Baldwin's writings. From it derives his talent for capturing in language the beauty and mystery of individual lives, from it too his often less than accomplished analysis of *issues* in his art. But a more significant implication of this sense of privacy is his clear preference for the 'biographical' treatment of characters and events. This biographical mood is progressively becoming impregnated by a more abstract perspective, but his published short stories (and especially 'Sonny's Blues') which were written during the early period of his career, serve as a useful illustration of this mood.

The stories in *Going to Meet the Man*[7] are quite representative, spanning, as they do, the scope of Baldwin's early thematic concerns. Both 'The Rockpile' and 'The Outing' deal in a rather summary fashion with two of his most recurrent themes, his memory of his brutal father and of his period in the church. These themes are to be found more elaborately presented in *Go Tell*, a novel of remembrance. As artistic creations, they are not of any great significance in themselves except in so far as they illustrate Baldwin's technical ability to achieve a coherence of language, theme, plot and structure when his subject is a familiar one. The third story in the collection, 'The ManChild,' is a rather curious one in the Baldwin corpus. It deals with the potential that misery and dispossession have for driving men into blind, pointless and motiveless brutality. Here, the malignity is not internalized or sublimated into a passionately vengeful religious fervour, nor is it objectified into a hatred of 'the man.' Rather, it is directed against one's closest friends. Jamie is a poor, luckless farmer whose only justification for living appears to be that of remaining a permanent drinking companion for Eric's father; and beneath all his exterior calm a vengefulness and hatred of Eric's father rages in him, later to manifest itself in infanticide. One interesting feature of this very short story is the banality of all the violence. The language is restrained, deliberately unelevated or emotional. The act of murder is itself reported

171

as though it were part of the normal events of any ordinary day. Jamie murders Eric in cold blood, apparently because he stands to inherit land from his father that used to belong to Jamie's own dad. Jamie, having strangled Eric, then walks back to his house as though nothing had happened, and it is in this contrived elemental triviality that the meaning of the story lies; beneath the 'normal' behaviour of Southern blacks who actually own and work their own land lurks a vicious and menacing brutality as terrifying as the more obvious violence of the Bigger Thomases of Northern ghettos.

'A Previous Condition,' touches upon a theme—the black artist's struggle for survival—that is later to be elaborated upon in *Tell Me*; 'This Morning, This Evening, So Soon' deals with the same theme, except that in this story the protagonist is an expatriate. 'Come into the Wilderness' is a tender story about a lonely black man from the South who has to work in New York, and a young black girl painfully in love with a white boy. In 'Going to Meet the Man,' Baldwin touches upon a theme that recurs in his works, namely, the close connection between the sexual inadequacies of white people in and out of power and their public reactions especially to young, virile black men. It is a theme that is later dramatized in *Blues for Mister Charlie*, Baldwin's play about race relations in the South. A distinguishing feature of this story is the devastating irony with which the author paints Jessie, the white deputy sheriff of the story. He is a self-righteous man who deliberately deludes himself into believing he is merely doing his duty when he defiles and brutalizes young black men and women. Yet ultimately, he is a figure more to be pitied than scorned. In a sense he is merely the hapless victim of a malevolent species of social determinism; he believes he is a true citizen only when, as his parents had done before him, he beats young black men and rapes black women. But the peculiar price he has to pay for his good citizenship is his impotence, his inability to maintain a healthy sexual relationship with his wife; for him the gun that lies beside his bed has become a veritable sexual organ, and only when he imagines he is raping a black girl can he effectively make love to his saintly wife. In the process of being a good law man, then, he becomes a dehumanized, sick, and dangerous human being. There is nothing hysterical about Baldwin's account of this sordid affair; there is a suspension of anger and rage that renders the story all the more forceful in its identification of the moral and psychological disease that lies at the core of racism.

None of these stories, however, demonstrates Baldwin's apparently effortless mastery of the short story form as 'Sonny's Blues' does. And this achievement derives not so much from the meaning of the story as from the manner in which nearly every word, every gesture in it, adds up toward the meeting of form, theme and meaning. One reason for this success is that the story is an intensely private one. The social conditions that make Sonny's choice necessary and meaningful are hardly ever mentioned. Rather, Baldwin appears to be more concerned to emphasize the psychic pain and the varying personal choices that two brothers make in order to accommodate a similar predicament—Sonny's brother (whose name is never mentioned) by opting for the safety that conformity brings (he is a High School teacher) and Sonny, by daring all and making his very pain the deep spring of his creative alienation.

In a quite significant sense the meaning of the story is to be found in its structure. To understand the way in which the blues operates as an art form is to discover its author's true intention in the story, for 'Sonny's Blues' is a song, and a moving one. Just as, in the blues, we do not usually find any profundities of thought, any events that are in themselves of cataclysmic import; just as through the almost ritualistic repetition of feeling, emotion and mood the blues singer achieves by a natural progression some revelatory insight into, and therefore some consolation for his pain, so also in this story the narrator's revelatory discovery in the end that there is something intrinsically valuable in Sonny's decision to be a musician is not sudden, nor is it the logical outcome of a set pattern of conflicting situations gradually resolving itself. As the narrator was himself to discover, there was nothing new either in Sonny's pain or in the infinite strategies that men must evolve to deal with their suffering:

Creole began to tell us what the blues were all about. They were not about anything very new. He and his boys up there were keeping it new, at the risk of ruin, destruction, madness, and death, in order to find new ways to make us listen. For, while the tale of how we suffer, and how we are delighted, and how we may triumph is never new, it always must be heard. There isn't any other tale to tell, it's the only light we've got in all this darkness.[8]

The song that must for ever be repeated, then, is the history of our journey through life, and the profit that we gain from it, as Ralph Ellison accurately observed, is not the consolation of philosophy, but the more visceral consolation that one derives from the numbing, oddly reassuring tediousness of everyday life. When the narrator begins his song, he immediately sets the pattern of shock and unhurried resolution that runs through the whole story:

> I read about it in the paper, in the subway, on my way to work. I read it, and I couldn't believe it, and I read it again. Then perhaps I just stared at it, at the newsprint spelling out his name, spelling out the story. I stared at it in the swinging lights of the subway car, and in the faces and bodies of the people, trapped in the darkness which roared outside.[9]

'Sonny's Blues' was written long before Baldwin's major works, and it gave sufficient indication of his technical ability to control the fictional form, but in many ways his greatest achievements were still to come, in the sixties when the pressure of political events and the dynamics of Baldwin's own personal history were to lead him into greater social involvement.

During the fifties, and despite the mood of his first published collection of essays, he might well have declared, with Joyce's Stephen Dedalus, that he would no longer serve that in which he no longer believed, whether it called itself his home, his fatherland, or his church. Certainly Baldwin himself has said enough about his life and thoughts during this period to make it clear that the prospect of active engagement in the shaping of social and political events was anathema to him. However, there was sufficient implicit evidence in his last two novels of a progressive, if halting radicalization, one that was to be more overtly expressed in his recent essay, *No Name in the Street*.

It is hardly necessary here to reiterate the historical circumstances that made this radicalization almost inevitable; it is more significant to observe that conditions both in Europe and America had led him to the conclusion that his sojourn in Paris was a faddish exhibition of 'elegant despair.' "Everybody else was paying their dues," he concluded, "and it was time I went home and paid mine." [10] *No Name in the Street* is Baldwin's long expected record of the dues he had to pay in the late fifties and sixties when he returned home from self-imposed exile and joined the Civil Rights Movement. In a sense, of course, *No Name* is an eloquent revisiting of the grounds of his equally moving apocalyptic prophecies of nine years ago. [In *The Fire Next Time* he had examined the evidence of America's moral corruption, of the monstrous racial injustices that threatened to plunge the nation into chaos, and his terrifying verdict had been that American civilization was recklessly bound on the road to utter oblivion. "If we do not now dare everything," he had then predicted, "the fulfilment of that prophecy, recreated from the Bible in song by a slave, is upon us: God gave Noah the rainbow sign, No more Water, the fire next time!"] At the time, many had been willing to congratulate him not only on the pristine intensity of his denunciations but also for having made it possible for them to feel complacent in the belief that an evil identified is an evil partially cured. The evidence adduced in this new essay is, however, compelling enough to make it quite clear that his predictions of disaster had largely fallen on deaf ears. "Who has believed our report," he asks, and the answer to that rhetorical question is, in the context in which it is asked, contained in the very exposition which Baldwin provides in his essay. In many ways, too, this essay comes from the same morally outraged consciousness as produced *The Fire Next Time*; there is in it the same determination to be the unsolicited voice of America's conscience, the same reluctance to advocate violent revolt as the 'logical' response to a situation that is by virtue of its very description glaringly intolerable. But Mel Watkins is obviously wrong when he mistakes this reluctance for a final failure to spell out the catastrophic alternatives

175

that the oppressed have at their disposal. Apart from the counsels of moral rectitude in *The Fire Next Time*, the fundamental weakness of that earlier essay derived from the all too apparent cleavage between analysis and conclusion,[11] between the 'logical' conclusions one is almost obliged to draw from the evidence adduced the eerily transcendental admonitions that Baldwin ends up with in that essay. And as Benjamin DeMott seems to believe, it may well have been that the exigencies of public spokesmanship made it inevitable that Baldwin should thus become merely the depersonalized recorder of the spirit of the times.[12]

We shall return to this issue later, but to argue, as Watkins does, that one derives only an 'implicit sense' of Baldwin's shift in perspective, to argue as he does that "nowhere in the essay is the judgment that Baldwin indicated he was forced into defined," [13] is to misunderstand the total meaning and implications of *No Name*. From the time of the publication of *Tell Me How Long the Train's Been Gone*, it had been clear that not only had Baldwin begun to achieve a long-awaited divorcement from the cosmology of sin and damnation, but that he was also becoming progressively more radical in the political sense of that term. The rise of Black Christopher in the Baldwin corpus was as dramatic an indication of this shift in ideological perspective as one could expect from so complex a mind, and even without the more authentic evidence of this last essay, it was from then on perfectly justifiable for us to assume that, theoretically at any rate, the rhetoric of violent confrontation was going to become an intrinsic part of his commitment. Consider, then, in light of this last remark, the following passage from *No Name*:

It is not necessary for a black man to hate a white man, or to have any particular feelings about him at all, in order to realise that he must kill him. Yes, we have come, or are coming to this, and there is no point in flinching before the prospect of this exceedingly cool species of fratricide. . . . Of course, whenever a black man discusses violence, he is said to be 'advocating' it. This is very far indeed from my intention; if only because I have no desire whatever to see a generation perish in the streets. But

176

the shape and extent of whatever violence may come is not in the hands of people like myself, but in the hands of the American people, who are at present among the most dishonorable and violent people in the world. I am merely trying to face certain blunt, human facts. I do not carry a gun and do not consider myself to be a violent man: but my life has more than once depended on the gun in a brother's holster. I know that when certain powerful and blatant enemies of black people are shoveled, at last, into the ground I may feel a certain pity . . . but I certainly do not mourn their passing, nor, when I hear that they are ailing, do I pray for their recovery. I know what I would do if I had a gun and someone had a gun pointed at my brother, and I would not count ten to do it and there would be no hatred in it, nor any remorse. People who treat other people as less than human must not be surprised when the bread they have cast on the waters comes floating back to them, poisoned.[14]

If the passage above is thought to be a little expansive, it is because we aim to suggest that it is one of the most crucial passages in the essay. It is a passage whose implications both for Baldwin's present state of mind and for the future of this country are terrifying indeed, and, as we shall suggest in a moment, to misunderstand the positive conclusions that can be derived from it is to fail to recognise the astute uses to which the Baldwinian rhetoric can be put.

Earlier in his essay Baldwin had referred to a 'something' that had altered in him, a change of mind he had gone through following the assassination of Martin Luther King; but the context of this statement had been such that it was not immediately clear what the precise nature of this change of mind had been, and for those, like Mel Watkins, who had expected a more closely organised 'paper,' Baldwin's failure immediately to satisfy our curiosity was no less than an indication of his incompetence and his now familiar preference for empty rhetoric. But nothing could be farther from the truth of the matter. It was not, for Baldwin, the *fact* of Dr. King's death that had disturbed him so much as the causes and the nature of his death. "Perhaps," he declared, "even more than the death itself, the manner of his death has forced me into a judgment concerning human life and human beings which I have always been reluctant to make;" [15] and at that point he had broken off his reflections on King's death and gone on to make general observations about human life which appeared to have only a vague connection to the 'judgment' he had come to. It is this deflection away from a concrete and specific declaration that Watkins presumably has in mind when he argues that Baldwin does not in his entire essay give us any but the most ambiguous idea of the judgment he had reached, and one can only suppose that his reading of this essay had been a hasty one. The passage above is, as a matter of fact, an almost perfect example of Baldwin's rhetorical skill. It does not merely state a deliberated conclusion; it not only elicits our rational consideration of the matter, but it also seeks to engage our emotional involvement by implying that the significance and enormity of the conclusion derives less from its logical inevitability than from the consideration that the writer has himself been extremely reluctant to come to it. Two specific remarks may here be made regarding this passage. First, Baldwin's intention appears to be to alert us to the 'fact' that violence is a logical response to social injustice, a violence that is all the more awesome because it is abstract and objective, having little to do with the emotions of those who engage in it. The particular attribute of this violence that makes it so repulsive to Baldwin and yet so compelling is its very divorcement from human emotion, its *abstractness*; observe the hesitancies, the deflections, the anxiety to postpone this catastrophe: "Yes, we have come, *or are coming to this;*" "I have no desire whatever to see a generation perish in the streets;" if this near-anthropomorphic 'violence' comes, "people like myself" will not be responsible for it. What Baldwin succeeds in doing here, then, through the personal qualifications, the alibis, is to bestow upon his 'judgment' an aura of objective inevitability without at the same time rendering it so abstract that it loses its immediacy—the emotional context in which it is actually stated. Secondly, the forcefulness of the passage derives as much from the suggested inevitability as from the concreteness of the language employed. There is a world of difference between calling the American people here 'dishonorable' and 'violent' and calling them 'immoral' or 'incapable of love,' as Baldwin did in *The Fire Next Time*; it is the difference between imagery that creates a sense of urgency and concrete immediacy and one that is grandiosely ambiguous and soporific. Ultimately, however, a less obvious function of this bluntness of language is to more specifically place the burden of guilt on 'white people' at the same time as it absolves Baldwin and 'people like him' from complicity in bringing about this terrible apocalypse.

No Name in the Street is, on the face of it, episodic, an impressionistic assessment of various personalities interspersed with narrative links that serve as foils to the portraits presented. But this apparent lack of structural organisation is deceptive. The essay opens with a now familiar autobiographical reference to Baldwin's childhood, but here the clear intention is to establish the essayist's identity—he is not only black, and therefore qualified to pass judgment on America, but he was also born in Harlem: both by virtue of his race and of his class origins, he is doubly dispossessed and therefore the eminently authentic voice of disbelief in a civilization that prides itself on its democratic and egalitarian mission. Having identified himself, Baldwin then tells us that at some point in his life he came to a certain altered judgment concerning the nature of human life, and we are not to have this judgment specified till the very last pages of the essay. The intervening space is then employed to present as many of the reasons that led to this altered judgment as are significant or representative, and it would be well here to examine some of these.

Mel Watkins is no doubt correct in identifying the paradoxical situation in which Baldwin found himself during the sixties. On the one hand, through his writings and public statements he had been one of the few Americans, certainly one of the first persuasive enough to evoke what was then thought to be a fundamental core of liberal idealism that was presumed to exist in the American psyche; through the unexceptionable moral authority of his positions he, with Dr. King, had been largely instrumental in creating that short-lived, euphoric age during which many were led to believe that the racial dilemma was one that could quite conceivably be resolved by untiring appeals to America's presumed sense of justice. Theirs was an 'act of faith' in the human capacity for moral perfection, but the paradox of the situation lay precisely here, that the extent of the failure and disillusionment of the Civil Rights Movement was exactly in proportion to the zeal and fervour with which Baldwin and King had appealed to the American people for a change of heart. As Baldwin was himself later to realise, the failure of the Movement was predictable, inherent in the logic of the circumstances themselves, because the Movement had been founded on a set of propositions that events later proved to have been imaginary. Baldwin here observes:

Part of the error was irreducible in that the marchers and petitioners were forced to suppose the existence of an entity which, when the chips were down, could not be located.

The liberal intellectuals since the days of McCarthy had been accustomed to indulge in "a masturbatory delusion," in "a wicked and dangerous fraud," and, in any case, there *were* no "American people" to appeal to; the Movement had been inspired by the compulsion "to demand of Americans—and for their sakes, after all—a generosity, a clarity, and a nobility which they did not dream of demanding of themselves," but the tribulations and failures of the Movement had led to the revelation that

. . . one could scarcely be deluded by Americans anymore, one scarcely dared expect anything from the great, vast, blank generality. . . . those descendants of a barbarous Europe who arbitrarily and arrogantly reserve the right to call themselves Americans.[16]

The disillusionments of the Movement of the sixties were in themselves devastating and traumatic enough to justify the reluctant but nonetheless definitive judgment at which Baldwin arrives at the end of this essay, but those who insist too much on the probability that he was merely a spokesman who articulated the spirit of the times in America might do well to reflect that the theatre of his political education went far beyond the shores of the American continent. If America, prior to the sixties, provided the emotional content of his judgment, its intellectual content came from a prolonged examination of the world situation. It was in France that he began to discover the dangers of international racism and to perceive the 'masturbatory delusions' of liberal intellectuals. He was in Paris during the fall of Dien Bien Phu, the consequent collapse of the French Empire in Indo-China, and the beginnings of the Algerian revolution. He had observed how the threat of the loss of empire and the resultant necessity for 'a radical revision of the individual identity' had led in France to an exacerbation of that menacing and vindictive brutality that had always been at the roots of colonialism.[17] He had also observed the behaviour of a large number of French intellectuals, and especially of Albert Camus (an Algerian by birth himself) for whom the concept of humanism "appeared to expire at the European gates: so that Camus, who was dedicated to liberty, in the case of Europeans, could only speak of 'justice' in the case of Algeria." [18] To be brief, Baldwin had long begun to observe the mannichean contradictions in Western idealism before he returned home, as he put it, to "pay his dues" in the Civil Rights Movement, and it must have occurred to him that the situation in America was hardly dissimilar to that in France or other European countries. Perhaps he felt the compulsion to search for pragmatic demonstration of his conclusions, and perhaps, too, he felt the need to justify his own sense of moral integrity through personal involvement. There is in any case no doubt that in going South he had exposed himself to terrifying dangers, and in addition to the more public conclusions that may be drawn from his record of the events of these tediously tragic years, it is probably equally significant to observe that out of this involvement he acquired a true sense of identity: what DeMott calls his 'pride.' "Perhaps," Baldwin was later to declare, "the moral of the story (and the hope of the world) lies in what one demands, not of others, but of oneself." [19]

If it is true, then, that Baldwin's involvement in the Civil Rights Movement was motivated less by faith in the moral responsibility of Americans than by a personal need both to test his conclusions in action and to justify his own sense of moral integrity, it seems a little meretricious for Watkins to insist that Baldwin's "ideological discourse is either too abstract and facile or too obvious to impress." [20] The fact of the matter is, first, that *No Name in the Street* embodies Baldwin's boldest excursion into the arena of specifically political analysis, and secondly, that in terms of his insight into the psycho-social perspective of the behaviour of Western man his remarks here are as valid and significant as those of more overtly political polemicists. Anyone nurtured on Fanonian dialectics or on the less profound disquisitions of many other twentieth century political analysts will no doubt be unlikely to be impressed by Baldwin's more impressionistic insights, but it is hardly necessary to observe that truth is not rendered insignificant by being obvious, nor any more profound by being esoteric. It is more instructive to observe, however, the manner in which Baldwin's world view encompasses the entire panorama of the politics of oppression. One does not often notice, for instance, in the writings of the more obvious Black American political theorists, the necessary distinction that Baldwin draws between the predicament of Algerians during the revolution and that of Black Americans here. Too often one reads and hears overly simplified analogies drawn between Fanon's theory of the colony and the condition of black people in this country. But as Baldwin makes it clear, while the Algerian struggle was invested with tragic dignity precisely because the Algerians were fighting for their land, one of the ironies in the situation here is that the fight for justice and freedom is based on propositions as theoretical and conceptualized as those that led to the famed revolution here two centuries ago. The point, of course, is not that the struggle here is any less obligatory or significant, but rather that the distinction which Baldwin attempts to draw is a crucial one:

(The Algerians) were not at home in Paris, no more than I, though for a different reason. They remembered, as it were, an opulence, opulence of taste, touch, water, sun, which I had barely dreamed of, and they had not come to France to stay. One day they were going home, and they knew exactly where home was. They, thus, held something within them which they would never surrender to France. But on my side of the ocean, or so it seemed to me then, we had surrendered everything, or had

182

had everything taken away, and there was no place for us to go: we *were* home.[21]

Baldwin's discovery of the significance of the 'territorial imperative' did not, however, prevent him from recognising the fundamental similarity between his dilemma and that of the Algerians. "The Algerians and I were both, alike, victims of this history, and I was still a part of Africa, even though I had been carried out of it nearly four hundred years before." The hard-headed realism of this observation is further demonstrated in his remarks on the regrettable but nonetheless necessary loss to human civilization that violence in the service of humanity brings with it. The great literary and intellectual contributions of European and American, as well as African and Asian writers and thinkers belong to mankind, but when these are employed as instruments of oppression they must be destroyed in the company of the more obvious paraphernalia of oppression:

> . . . in order to be rid of Shell, Texaco, Coca-Cola, the Sixth Fleet, and the friendly American soldier whose mission it is to protect these investments, one finally throws Balzac and Shakespeare—and Faulkner and Camus—out with them. Later, of course, one may welcome them back, but on one's own terms, and, absolutely, on one's own land.[22]

The practical wisdom of such a political strategy may, of course, be open to question; it may be well to ask if it is in fact possible to accept any of the above agents of colonialism on 'one's own terms,' but we would not be exaggerating if we observed that it is very seldom that revolutionary commentators of the twentieth century have deemed it necessary to deal squarely with this problem. To the extent, therefore, that Baldwin was prepared to risk criticism on so crucial and vexatious an issue, he must, it seems to us, be given credit for his rather unusual readiness to plunge himself into the very thick of ideological controversy.

Baldwin's sense of personal integrity has never really been in question; the moral authority of his admonitions and prophecies has often derived as much from the 'truth' of his observations as from one's knowledge that he, after all, was as authentic an American as 'citizen Paine' ever was. As he himself has often observed, it is precisely because of his stake in the health of America that he has reserved for himself the right to denounce as vehemently as possible the moral corruption of its polity. And with the rhetorical equipment he inherited from the Black Church, few have succeeded as he has done in describing with seriousness, passion and urgency the plight of the oppressed or the moral predicament of American civilization. Let us cite here, as illustration, a passage in which eloquence and rage coalesce to produce a brilliance both of vision and of language that is clearly outstanding:

> I do not claim that everyone in prison here is innocent, but I do claim that the law, as it operates, is guilty, and that the prisoners, therefore, are all unjustly imprisoned. Is it conceivable . . . that any middle-class white boy—or, indeed, almost any white boy— would have been arrested on so grave a charge as murder, with such flimsy substantiation, and forced to spend, as of this writing, three years in prison? What force, precisely, is operating when a prisoner is advised, requested, ordered, intimidated, or forced, to confess to a crime he has not committed, and promised a lighter sentence for so perjuring and debasing himself? Does the law exist for the purpose of furthering the ambitions of those who have sworn to uphold the law, or is it seriously to be considered as a moral, unifying force, the health and strength of a nation? . . . If one really wished to know how justice is administered in a country, one does not question the policemen, the lawyers, the judges, or the protected members of the middle-class. One goes to the unprotected—those, precisely, who need the law's protection most!—and listens to their testimony. Ask any Mexican, any Puerto Rican, any black man, any poor person—ask the wretched how they fare in the halls of justice, and then you will know, not whether or not the country is just, but whether or not it has any love for justice, or any concept of it. It

is certain, in any case, that ignorance, allied with power, is the most ferocious enemy justice can have.[23]

This, then, is the record of a writer who for a long time struggled to fashion out of the turmoil of his own private history and the turbulence of social and political affairs in our time a public voice that was as much dignified as it was terrifying. At the point when James Baldwin declared in *No Name in the Street*—"I know what I would do if I had a gun"—it was clear that he had come a long way from the days when he appeared preoccupied with the 'theological terror' that he saw as implicit in Harriet Beecher Stowe's novel. In his long and painful journey to the gates of the secular city he had lost something of the structural precision that had been a distinguishing characteristic of his earlier novels. But for this loss, we believe, there was much greater recompense. Once he began to make his fiction and his essays the vehicle for the expression of his own sense of moral disgust and passionate fury, he attained a place in the history of American letters that few so far can claim in this century. He is now forty-eight, a rather young man as writers go, and there is reason to believe that now that he has found his authentic voice —a voice in which the man and the writer no longer contend for primacy—he will again recapture that mastery of the fictional form of which he had given such distinguished evidence in *Go Tell It on the Mountain*. It would be folly, indeed almost indecent, to recite in so provisional an assessment, a litany of his achievements so far; for that the reader must search the pages of other works. The one thing that is certain at this point in time is that James Baldwin, from the inner resources strained from an unlikely heritage and an even more improbable environment, is a major writer, and were we under some obligation to pass some final judgment on his achievement, we would only say, paraphrasing him, that he was a 'good' writer long before he found a fit subject to write about, and though it took him a long time, he is now in the process of becoming an 'honest man.' And it is not inconceivable that he may finally—so inexorable is the logic of the thing itself—come to the conclusion that the limitations of art are too intolerable for anyone who dares

185

to be an honest man in an age of moral ambiguity, and, with the hordes of the dispossessed, take up arms against his sea of troubles.

Notes to Chapter Eight

1. See, e.g., Henry H. Mitchell, *Black Preaching*, for a summary of the rhetorical characteristics of the black sermon.
2. See Chapters Three and Five
3. See John Weightman's useful essay on Alain Robbe-Grillet in *The New York Review of Books*, Vol. XVIII, No. 10, June 1, 1972, pp. 6–10
4. See, e.g., Hoyt Fuller, 'Toward a Black Aesthetic,' in Addison Gayle, Jr., ed., *The Black Aesthetic*, Doubleday, 1971, pp. 3–12
5. See, Marcus Klein, *After Alienation: American Novels in Mid-Century*, Cleveland, World, 1964, for his reading of Baldwin's essays
6. Baldwin, *No Name in the Street*, Dial, 1972, p. 172
7. Baldwin, *Going to Meet the Man*, Dell, 1965
8. Baldwin, 'Sonny's Blues,' *Going to Meet the Man*, p. 121
9. ibid. p. 86
10. Baldwin, *No Name in the Street*, p. 50
11. See Chapter One
12. Benjamin DeMott, Review of *No Name*, Saturday Review, May 27, 1972, p. 63
13. Mel Watkins, Review of *No Name*, New York Times Review of Books, May 28, 1972, p. 18
14. Baldwin, *No Name*, pp. 191–92
15. ibid., p. 9
16. ibid., pp. 10, 31, passim
17. ibid., p. 25
18. ibid., p. 43
19. ibid., p. 10
20. Watkins, op. cit., p. 17
21. Baldwin, *No Name*, p. 24
22. ibid., p. 48
23. ibid., pp. 148–49

Selected Bibliography

A. Bibliographies:

Fisher, Russell G, 'James Baldwin: A Bibliography, 1947–62,' *Bulletin of Bibliography*, IV (1965)

Kindt, Kathleen A, 'James Baldwin: A Checklist, 1947–62', *Bulletin of Bibliography*, XXIV (1965)

Turner, Darwin T, *Bibliography of Afro-American Writers*, Appleton-Century-Crofts, 1970

B. Works by James Baldwin, arranged chronologically:

Go Tell It on the Mountain, first published by Alfred Knopf, 1953
Notes of a Native Son, first published by Beacon, 1955
Giovanni's Room, Dial, 1956
Nobody Knows My Name, Dial, 1961
Another Country, Dial, 1963
The Fire Next Time, Dell, 1962
Blues for Mister Charlie, Dial, 1964
Going to Meet the Man, Dial, 1965
Tell Me How Long the Train's Been Gone, Dial, 1967
The Amen Corner, Dial, 1968
A Rap on Race (with Margaret Mead), London, 1971
No Name in the Street, Dial, 1972

C. Books:

(i) Biographies:
Eckman, Fern Marja, *The Furious Passage of James Baldwin*, M. Evans, 1966
(ii) Others:
Allen, Walter, *The Modern Novel in Britain and the United States*, Dutton, 1964
Baker, Houston A, ed. *Black Literature in America*, McGraw Hill, 1971
Bennett, LeRone, *The Negro Mood*, Chicago, Johnson, 1965
Berrian, Albert H, and Richard A. Long, eds. *Negritude: Essays and Studies*, Hampton Institute Press, 1967
Bigsby, C. E. ed. *The Black American Writer: Volume 1, Fiction*, Florida, E. Edwards, 1969
Bone, Robert A, *The Negro Novel in America*, rev. ed. Yale, 1965

Broderick, Francis, and A. Meier, eds. *Negro Protest Thought in the Twentieth Century*, Indianapolis, Bobbs-Merrill, 1965

Brown, Claude, *Manchild in the Promised Land*, Macmillan, 1965

Butcher, Margaret, *The Negro in American Culture*, A. Knopf, 1956

Clark, Kenneth, *Dark Ghetto*, Harper and Row, 1965

Clarke, John Henrik, *William Styron's Nat Turner: Ten Black Writers Respond*, Beacon, 1969

Charters, Samuel B, *The Poetry of the Blues*, Oak Press, 1963

Cleaver, Eldridge, *Soul on Ice*, Dell, 1968

Cone, James, *Black Theology and Black Power*, Seabury, 1970

Cronon, Edmund D, *Black Moses: The Story of Marcus Garvey and the Universal Negro Improvement Association*, Madison, University of Wisconsin Press, 1955

Cruse, Harold, *The Crisis of the Negro Intellectual*, Apollo, 1967

Ellison, Ralph, *Shadow and Act*, Random House, 1964

Fiedler, Leslie A, *Love and Death in the American Novel*, Stein and Day, 1966

Frazier, E. Franklin, *The Negro Church in America*, Shocken, 1963

Gayle, Addison, *The Black Aesthetic*, Doubleday, 1971

Gibson, Donald B, ed. *Five Black Writers*, New York University Press, 1970

Harper, Howard, *Desperate Faith: A Study of Bellow, Salinger, Mailer, Baldwin and Updike*, University of North Carolina Press, 1969

Hassan, Ihab, *Radical Innocence*, Princeton, 1961

Hernton, Calvin, *White Papers for White Americans*, Doubleday, 1966

Jones, LeRoi, *Blues People: Negro Music in White America*, Morrow, 1963

———, *Home: Social Essays*, Morrow, 1966

Karlen, Arno, *Sexuality and Homosexuality: A New View*, W. W. Norton, 1971

Kazin, Alfred, *Contemporaries*, Boston, Little, Brown, 1962

Klein, Marcus, *After Alienation: American Novels in Mid-Century*, Cleveland, World, 1964

Killens, John O, *Black Man's Burden*, Trident, 1965

Lewis, David, *King: A Critical Biography*, Praeger, 1970

Mailer, Norman, *Advertisements for Myself*, Putnam, 1959

———, *The Armies of the Night*, Signet, 1968

Margolies, Edward, *Native Sons: A Critical Study of Twentieth Century Negro American Authors*, J. B. Lippincott, 1968

Miller, Ruth, ed. *Black American Literature*, Beverly Hills, 1971

Moore, Harry, ed. *Contemporary American Novelists*, Southern Illinois University Press, 1964

Podhoretz, Norman, *Doings and Undoings*, Farrar, Straus, 1964

Redding, Saunders, *On Being Negro in America*, Indianapolis, Bobbs-Merrill, 1965

Sontag, Susan, *Styles of Radical Will*, Farrar, Straus, 1969

Williams, John A, *The King God Didn't Save*, Coward McCann, 1970

———, *The Man Who Cried I Am*, Signet, 1967

Wright, Richard, *White Man, Listen*, Doubleday, 1957

D. *Articles, Essays, Reviews:*

Algren, Nelson, 'Lost Man,' *Nation*, CLXXXIII, 1956

Barksdale, Richard K, 'Temple of the Fire Baptized,' *Phylon*, XIV, 1953

Bigby, C. W, 'The Committed Writer: James Baldwin as Dramatist,' *Twentieth Century Literature*, XIII, 1967

Bonosky, Phillip, 'The Negro Writer and Commitment,' *Mainstream*, XV, 1962

Bradford, Melvin E, 'Faulkner, James Baldwin and the South,' *Georgia Review*, XX, 1962

Cartey, Wilfred, 'The Realities of Four Negro Writers,' *Columbia University Forum Anthology*, IX, iii, 1966

Charney, Maurice, 'James Baldwin's Quarrel with Richard Wright,' *American Quarterly*, XV, 1963 •

Coles, Robert, 'Baldwin's Burden,' *Partisan Review*, XXXI, 1964

Collier, Eugenia, 'The Phrase Unbearably Repeated,' *Phylon*, XXV, 1964

———, 'Thematic Patterns in Baldwin's Essays,' *Black World*, June, 1972

Cox, C. B. and A. R. Jones, 'After the Tranquilized Fifties: Notes on Sylvia Plath and James Baldwin,' *Critical Quarterly*, VI, 1964

DeMott, Benjamin, 'James Baldwin on the Sixties: Acts and Revelations,' *Saturday Review*, May 27, 1972

Esty, William, 'The Cities of the Plain,' *New Republic*, CXXXV, Dec. 17, 1956

Finn, James, 'James Baldwin's Vision,' *Commonweal*, LXXVII, 1962

Flint, R. W, 'Not Ideas But Life,' *Commentary*, XXI, 1956

Gayle, Addison, 'A Defense of Baldwin,' *CLA Journal*, X, 1966

Gerard, Albert, 'Humanism and Negritude: Notes on the Contemporary Afro-American Novel,' tr. S. Alexander, *Diogenes*, No. 37, Spring, 1962

Goodman, Paul, 'Not Enough of a World to Grow In,' *New York Times Book Rev.* June 24, 1964

Graves, Wallace, 'The Question of Moral Energy in James Baldwin's *Go Tell It on the Mountain*,' *CLA Journal*, VII, 1963

Gross, Theodore, 'The World of James Baldwin,' *Critique*, VII, ii, 1965

Hassan, Ihab, 'The Novel of Outrage: A Minority Voice in Post War American Fiction,' *American Scholar*, XXXIV, 1965

Hicks, Granville, 'Commitment Without Compromise,' *Saturday Review*, XLIV, July 1, 1961

———, 'Outcasts in a Cauldron of Hate,' *Saturday Review*, XIV, July 7, 1962

Hoffman, Stanton, 'The Cities of Night: John Rechy's *City of Night* and the American Literature of Homosexuality,' *Critical Review*, XVII, ii–iii, 1964

Hughes, Langston, 'From Harlem to Paris,' *New York Times*, Feb. 26, 1956

Illo, John, 'The Rhetoric of Malcolm X,' *Columbia Univ. Forum Anthology*, IX, iii, 1966, ed. Peter Spackman

Isaacs, H. R, 'Five Writers and their African Ancestors,' *Phylon*, XXI, 1960

Jacobson, D, 'James Baldwin as Spokesman,' *Commentary*, XXXII, 1961

Jones, Lawrence, 'Black Churches in Historical Perspective,' *Christianity and Crisis: A Journal of Christian Opinion*, Vol. XXX, No. 18, Nov. 2 & 16, 1970

Karp, David, 'A Squalid World,' *Saturday Review*, XXXIX, Dec. 1, 1956

Kent, George, 'Baldwin and the Problem of Being,' *CLA Journal*, VII, 1964

Lash, John S, 'Baldwin Beside Himself: A Study in Modern Phalicism,' *CLA Journal*, VIII, 1964

MacInnes, Colin, 'Dark Angel: The Writings of James Baldwin,' *Encounter*, XXI, Aug. 1963

Malcolm, D, 'The Author in Search of Himself,' *New Yorker*, XXXVII, Nov. 25, 1961

Marcus, Steven, 'The American Negro in Search of Identity,' *Commentary*, XVI, 1953

189

Mayfield, Julian, 'Love Affair with the United States,' *New Republic*, CXLV, Aug. 7, 1967

Newman, Charles, 'The Lesson of the Master: Henry James and James Baldwin,' *Yale Review*, LVI, 1966

O'Daniel, Therman B, 'James Baldwin: An Interpretive Study,' *CLAJ*, VII, 1963

Rainer, Dachine, 'Rage into Order,' *Commonweal*, LXIII, 1956

Sheares, Reuben, 'Beyond White Theology,' *Christianity and Crisis*, No. 18, Nov. 2 & 16, 1970

Spender, Stephen, 'James Baldwin: Voice of a Revolution,' *Partisan Review*, XXX, 1963

Trilling, Lionel, 'The Fate of Pleasure,' in Sheldon Grebstein, ed., *Perspectives in Contemporary Criticism*, Harper and Row, 1968

Watkins, Mel, 'The Fire Next Time This Time,' *New York Times Book Review*, May 28, 1972

Index

191